D0822078

GREENWICH LIBRARIES
3 8028 00918556 9

SCEPTRE

Sceptre

SCEPTRE

The Seventeenth Challenger

---

by

HUGH SOMERVILLE

CASSELL · LONDON

CASSELL & COMPANY LTD
35 Red Lion Square
London W.C. 1

and at
210 Queen Street, Melbourne
26/30 Clarence Street, Sydney
24 Wyndham Street, Auckland
1068 Broadview Avenue, Toronto 6
P.O. Box 275, Cape Town
P.O. Box 11190, Johannesburg
Haroon Chambers, South Napier Road, Karachi
13/14 Ajmeri Gate Extension, New Delhi 1
15 Graham Road, Ballard Estate, Bombay 1
17 Chittaranjan Avenue, Calcutta 13
P.O. Box 23, Colombo
Denmark House (3rd Floor), 84 Ampang Road, Kuala Lumpur
Avenida 9 de Julho 1138, São Paulo
Galeria Güemes, Escritorio 454/59 Florida 165, Buenos Aires
Marne 5b, Mexico 5, D.F.
Sanshin Building, 6 Kanda Mitoschiro-cho, Chiyoda-ku, Tokyo
97 rue Monge, Paris 5e
25 Ny Strandvej, Espergaerde, Copenhagen
Beulingstraat 2, Amsterdam-C
Bederstrasse 51, Zürich 2

First published 1958

PRINTED IN GREAT BRITAIN BY
EBENEZER BAYLIS AND SON, LTD., THE TRINITY PRESS
WORCESTER, AND LONDON
F.958

Contents

Acknowledgements

In writing this book I have been very fortunate in having the blessing as well as the help and encouragement of Mr. Hugh Goodson and the eleven other gallant gentlemen who owned the Seventeenth Challenger. I am also indebted to countless others, who assisted with the building and equipment of *Sceptre*, and who gave me help and advice. As far as possible I have mentioned in the text the part played by each.

I should particularly like to thank Lieutenant-Colonel R. S. G. Perry, Owen Aisher, Charles Grattan, G. Colin Ratsey, Frank J. Murdoch, the Brooks brothers, Derek Woods, Graham Mann, and Stanley Bishop, as well as many other members of the crews of *Sceptre* and *Evaine*. David Boyd was kind enough to spare me a Sabbath afternoon in midwinter, as well as allowing me to wander round his yard at will in the later stages. Jim Macaulay kindly let me have the admirably clear drawings in Appendixes D and E, and was also responsible, with David Boyd, for the exquisite cutaway perspective drawing between pages 100 and 101. I am indebted to W. A. Crago, Tanks Superintendent of Saunders-Roe, Ltd., for the notes and photographs concerning the tank tests, and for allowing me to watch them.

The photographers have been most helpful, notably William Yuile, Frank and Keith Beken, and Morris Rosenfeld and his sons.

For the historical section I have had to draw on the experience of others. Sir Thomas Sopwith spared me an hour of his valuable time. I also wish to acknowledge my indebtedness for information obtained from the following reference books: *British Yachts and Yachtsmen* (*The Yachtsman*, 1908), *The Lawson History of the* America's *Cup* (1902), *Further*

Memorials of the Royal Yacht Squadron, J. B. Atkins (Bles 1939), *Racing for the* America*'s Cup*, Lieutenant-Commander P. K. Kemp (Hutchinson 1937).

For permission to use copyright material I must thank the Editor of *The Yachting Monthly*, Harold S. Vanderbilt and Charles Scribners' Sons, New York, *On the Wind's Highway* (copyright 1939). Sherman Hoyt and D. Van Nostrand Company Inc., Sherman Hoyt's *Memoirs* (copyright 1950), and the same company for permission to quote from *Clinton Crane's Yachting Memoirs.*

While at Newport, R.I., I received much valuable help from Bill Wallace of the *New York Herald Tribune* and Norris D. Hoyt. Last but not least, Miss M. Cuff typed much of an often almost illegible manuscript.

Illustrations

THE frontispiece, the photographs of *America*, *Genesta* and *Rex*, *Valkyrie II*, the *Endeavours*, *Vim*, and *Evaine* between pages 36 and 37, the photographs of *Sceptre* and *Evaine* together, and Colonel Perry at the wheel of *Evaine* between pages 100 and 101, are reproduced by permission of Beken & Son, Cowes.

The photographs of *Ranger*, and of *Gleam*, *Nyala*, and *Vim* practising together are reproduced by permission of Morris Rosenfeld, New York.

Saunders-Roe provided the tank test photographs; *The Times* the photographs of the christening and *Sceptre*'s galley and cockpit; Vista of Glasgow the working shot of *Sceptre*'s rudder heel; James Hall, Ltd., the reeving of the jib halyard tail; and Eric Stewart the making of one of *Sceptre*'s mainsails.

PART ONE

THE HISTORY

I

1851 to 1887—The First Races and the Deeds of Gift

ON the gloomy evening of 22nd August 1851 a schooner called *America* crossed the finishing line at Cowes to win the Royal Yacht Squadron £100 Cup which now bears her famous name. She was owned by a syndicate of members of the New York Yacht Club, headed by Commodore John C. Stevens, the others being Edwin Stevens, George L. Schuyler, Colonel James Hamilton, J. Beekman Finley, and Hamilton Wilkes.

America had sailed across the Atlantic at the invitation of the Earl of Wilton, Commodore of the Royal Yacht Squadron. It was the year of the Great Exhibition and her owners hoped for plenty of racing, good prize money, special matches, and large cash wagers. They were disappointed. Apart from the Cup race, *America* sailed only one more, a match against the schooner *Titania* for £100. British yachtsmen were deterred by the way in which she outsailed the cutter *Laverock*, which had gone out to meet her, on her way over from Havre, after her transatlantic voyage.

The tale of the race eastabout round the Isle of Wight, which *America* won from fifteen of the best British yachts, has been told many times. It started at ten o'clock from anchor in two lines, the cutters a cable and a half ahead of the schooners. *America* was last away, but had climbed to fifth place when she reached the Nab Tower. There was a muddle over the course, an event not unknown even in these days, some boats rounding the Nab, leaving it to starboard, but

America went inside, leaving it to port. A protest against her on those grounds was dismissed. One of her rivals, *Arrow*, ran ashore and *Alarm* stood by her. Off Ventnor *Volante* and *Freak* fouled each other. These two boats had been ahead of *America*, so the incident gave her the lead, which she increased on the beat from St. Catherine's Point to the Needles. As she ran up the West Solent she was met by the Royal Yacht *Victoria and Albert*, with Queen Victoria aboard. The American schooner was several miles ahead of her nearest rival, *Aurora*, and it was at this stage that the legendary report, '*America* first, Your Majesty. There is no second', is supposed to have been made by her signalman, reporting to the Queen. There is a theory that in fact the report was made by Daniel Webster about a fortnight later, when he broke off a speech to make it at a celebration in Boston to mark the opening of the railway between the U.S.A. and the Canadian provinces.

In actual fact *Aurora*, a 47-tonner, had come up fast in the light air and only finished 21 minutes astern of *America*. As the latter displaced 170 tons, she would almost certainly have been beaten had any known form of handicapping been used.

The race against *Titania* followed on 28th August, *America* winning by 52 minutes over a course 20 miles to windward and back, in spite of breaking her foregaff.

The design of Commodore Stevens's schooner differed from that of contemporary British yachts. She was a New York pilot-boat model, with a very fine entry, her greatest beam well aft, a broad stern and a very vee'd midship section. Her masts were well raked, but probably the most important feature was her fine sails. These were made of cotton, laced to the boom and cut very flat, whereas the English boats had loose-footed, baggy, flax sails.

As the syndicate could find no more racing they sold her in England to the Hon. John de Blaquière for £4,000, and returned to the U.S.A. with the Cup and £100. Precious little really seems to have been learned from her by British designers and sailmakers of that time. Indeed, while under British ownership she was equipped with loose-footed hempen sails and her rig was cut down. She was also rebuilt, which helped to preserve her until she was broken up in 1952.

The Cup, sometimes erroneously described as the Queen's Cup, reposed in Commodore Stevens's house in Washington Square until 1857. In July of that year he and the four survivors of the syndicate offered it to the New York Yacht Club as a permanent challenge trophy. The letter offering it and the conditions governing it were as follows:

New York, July 8, 1857.

To the Secretary of the New York Yacht Club:

Sir,

The undersigned, members of the New York Yacht Club, and late owners of the schooner yacht *America*, beg leave through you to present to the Club the Cup won by the *America* at the Regatta of the Royal Yacht Squadron at Cowes, England, August 22, 1851.

This cup was offered as a prize to be sailed for by yachts of all nations without regard to differences of tonnage, going round the Isle of Wight, the usual course for the Annual Regatta of the Royal Yacht Squadron, and was won by the *America*, beating eight cutters and seven schooner yachts which started in the race.

The Cup is offered to the New York Yacht Club, subject to the following conditions:

Any organised Yacht Club of any foreign country shall always be entitled, through any one or more of its members to claim the right of sailing a match for this Cup with any yacht or other vessel of not less than 30 or more than 300 tons, measured by the Custom House rule of the country to which the vessel belongs.

The parties desiring to sail for the Cup may make any match with the Yacht Club in possession of the same that may be determined upon by mutual consent, but in case of disagreement as to terms, the match shall be sailed over the usual course for the Annual Regatta of the Yacht Club in possession of the Cup, and subject to the Rules and Sailing Regulations, the challenging party being bound to give six months' notice in writing, fixing the day on which they wish to start. This notice to embrace the length, Custom House measurement, rig and name of the vessel.

It is to be distinctly understood that the Cup is to be the property of the Club, and not of the members thereof, or owners of the vessels winning it in a match; and that the condition of keeping it open to be sailed for by Yacht Clubs of all foreign countries, upon the terms above laid down, shall forever attach to it, thus making it a perpetual Challenge Cup for friendly competition between foreign countries.

J. C. STEVENS
EDWIN A. STEVENS
HAMILTON WILKES
J. BEEKMAN FINLEY
GEORGE L. SCHUYLER

These terms were announced by the New York Yacht Club to all the Yacht Clubs of the world. No one was interested until 1868 when Mr. James Ashbury, Vice-Commodore of the Royal Harwich Yacht Club, wrote to the New York Yacht Club. He was the owner of the schooner *Cambria*, which had raced with success against the American schooner *Sappho* in British waters that year. He suggested that the New York Y.C. chose their best schooner of a tonnage of not more than 206·8 (i.e. ten per cent more than his *Cambria*) to come across the Atlantic to race in the 1869 British regattas. *Cambria* and this schooner would race back across the Atlantic for a £250 silver trophy. They would then sail three matches under time allowance calculated under the Royal Thames Y.C. rule, the winner of two of them to hold the *America*'s Cup.

This was not what Commodore Stevens and his friends contemplated, and a wrangling correspondence followed, which brought the Cup back into the public eye. Mr. Ashbury objected to centreboard yachts. So, when the challenge with

Cambria was sent from the Royal Harwich Y.C., on 14th November 1869, he sought to introduce as a condition a Royal Yacht Squadron rule excluding such craft.

For *Cambria's* passage across the Atlantic a race was organized against the crack American ocean racer *Dauntless*, owned by James Gordon Bennett, which had been cruising in European waters. They started on 4th July 1870 from Daunt Rock in Ireland and *Cambria* crossed the line off Sandy Hook 23 days 5 hours and 17 minutes later, winning by 1 hour and 43 minutes.

The only race for the cup was between *Cambria* and twenty American yachts. As these included sixteen centreboard boats, it is obvious that Mr. Ashbury's attempt to bar them had been ignored, as had been his suggestion of the best of three races.

Cambria was given the windward berth on the starting line of the New York Y.C. course with the old *America* next to her. The latter, now back in American hands, had been refitted and manned by the U.S. Navy. The enormous spectator fleet surprised even the Americans.

The wind shifted just before the start, so *Cambria* found herself to leeward. She was badly blanketed and finished eighth, 27 minutes 3 seconds behind the schooner *Magic*, being placed tenth on corrected time. *America* was fourth.

Mr. Ashbury returned to England in December 1870 and immediately ordered a new schooner from Michael Ratsey of Cowes, who had designed and built *Cambria*. While the latter was a typical British schooner, *Livonia*, as the new challenger was called, was as near the American type as her designer could make her. She was no better than *Cambria*, but Mr. Ashbury thought she would do better in American conditions.

Livonia's sail area was 18,153 square feet, the greatest ever carried by a Cup challenger and nearly ten times that of a Twelve Metre of the present Cup race class.

During the early summer of 1871 Mr. Ashbury kept up a lengthy correspondence which tended to get acrimonious, and in the course of it he tried to challenge from twelve different clubs! It had the effect of making the contest a series of seven match-races, although the New York Y.C. reserved the right to nominate one of four defenders each day. The courses were alternately the New York Y.C. course and 20 miles to windward and return off Sandy Hook, the first race being on 16th October.

Columbia beat *Livonia* in the first two races, but lost the third because her steering gear failed. She was replaced by *Sappho*, which won the next two, and the Cup. This was not quite the end.

After the second race Mr. Ashbury had protested against *Columbia* on the grounds that she had left the mark to port. *Livonia* had left it to starboard, which entailed a gybe, by which she lost considerably from her opponent who had tacked. No side was specified in the sailing instructions and the New York Y.C. ruled that in such a case it was optional. Mr. Ashbury did not accept the ruling. (The English rules of that time laid it down that in such a case it should be left to starboard.) He considered that his protest made the score three races to two, with two to sail. He told the Club that he would sail these remaining two races and claim the cup, which indeed he tried to do, although he only sailed round once. He then went home threatening to bring his lawyer if he ever challenged for the cup again.

He must have been a rather cantankerous gentleman, but to give him his due he was instrumental in making the cup races fairer. Never again did the New York Y.C. nominate one of several defenders on the day of the race. There was little interest in England after Mr. Ashbury's second defeat, and he became M.P. for Harwich and never challenged again.

In 1876 the Royal Canadian Y.C. challenged with the *Countess of Dufferin*, owned by a syndicate headed by Major Charles Gifford, the Vice-Commodore. They insisted on racing against a single defender nominated by the New York Y.C. before the first race, to which the latter agreed. The challenger was an American type schooner, with a centreboard, but the syndicate suffered from lack of money. She was in poor shape and was easily beaten by the schooner *Madelaine*, owned by John S. Dickerson, Commodore of the Brooklyn Y.C. The challenger was sold in the Sheriff's Court to satisfy a creditor's claim, but Alexander Cuthbert, the largest shareholder, was determined to challenge again.

He did so in the name of the Bay of Quinte Yacht Club, on Lake Ontario, with a cutter called *Atalanta*. He was backed by a syndicate and he designed and built the challenger himself, sailing with an amateur crew against the iron sloop *Mischief*. She was owned by an Englishman, J. R. Busk, who was a New York Y.C. member, a selection which, as can be imagined, did not meet with universal approval in the U.S.A. *Atalanta* was easily beaten and after the races were over the New York Y.C. returned the Cup to Mr. George L. Schuyler, the last survivor of the *America* syndicate, who produced a new Deed of Gift, dated 2nd February 1882, which is reproduced below:

SECOND DEED OF GIFT

Any organised yacht club of a foreign country, incorporated, patented or licensed by the Legislature, Admiralty or other executive department, having for its annual regatta an ocean water course on the sea or on an arm of the sea (or one which combines both), practicable for vessels of 300 tons, shall always be entitled, through one or more of its members, to the right of sailing a match for this Cup, with a yacht or other vessel propelled by sails only, and constructed in the country to which the challenging club belongs, against any one yacht or vessel as aforesaid, constructed in the country of the club holding the Cup.

The yacht or vessel is to be of not less than 30 or more than 300 tons, measured by the Custom House rule in use by the country of the challenging party.

The challenging party shall give six months' notice in writing, naming the day for the proposed race, which day shall not be later than seven months from the date of the notice.

The parties intending to sail for the Cup may, by mutual consent, make any arrangement satisfactory to both as to the date, course, time allowance, number of trials, rules, and sailing regulations, and any and all other conditions of the match, in which case the six months' notice may be waived.

In case the parties cannot mutually agree upon the terms of the match, then the challenging party shall have the right to contest for the Cup in one trial, sailed over the usual course of the annual regatta of the club holding the Cup, subject to its rules and sailing regulations, the challenged party not being required to name its representative until the time agreed upon for the start.

Accompanying the six months' notice, there must be a Custom House certificate of the measurement, and a statement of the dimensions, rig, and name of the vessel.

No vessel which has been defeated in a match for this Cup can be again selected by any club for its representative until after the contest for it by some other vessel has intervened, or until after the expiration of two years from the time such contest has taken place.

Vessels intending to compete for this Cup must proceed under sail on their own bottoms to the port where the contest is to take place.

Should the club holding the Cup be for any cause dissolved, the Cup shall be handed over to any club of the same nationality it may select, which comes under the foregoing rules.

It is to be distinctly understood that the Cup is to be the property of the club and not of the owners of the vessel winning it in a match, and that the condition of keeping it open to be sailed for by organised yacht clubs of all foreign countries, upon the terms above laid down, shall forever attach to it, thus making it perpetually a challenge Cup for friendly competition between foreign countries.

GEORGE L. SCHUYLER

As can be seen, it laid down that the challenger would meet 'any one yacht. . . .' and so removed the cause of much bitterness. The defeated yacht could not try again until another series had been sailed or two years had elapsed, and the challenger had to sail to the races on her own bottom. This was designed to prevent a yacht being towed, as *Atalanta* was, through the Erie Canal. The challenging Club had to hold its annual regatta over a sea course, and so it infuriated the Canadians, against whom it was directed.

As before, the New York Y.C. sent a copy to all foreign yacht clubs, but despite various rumours, nothing happened until 1884, when an English designer, J. Beavor Webb, intimated that two challenges were to be made by yachts of his design. The first, from the Royal Yacht Squadron, with Sir Richard Sutton's *Genesta*, and the second by the Royal Northern Yacht Club with another cutter, *Galatea*, owned by Lieutenant William Henn, R.N.

Mr. Webb was anxious for British time allowances to be used, but Mr. Schuyler ruled in favour of the time allowances of the Club in possession. The New York Y.C. agreed to forgo the stipulated six month's notice, should *Genesta*'s challenge fail, and the series were to consist of three races, one over the New York Y.C. inside course and the other two off Sandy Hook.

Both *Genesta* and *Galatea* were typical British 'plank on edge' type of boats, which had been encouraged by the Royal Thames Y.C. tonnage rule, which penalizes beam. The effect of this rule is still felt today as many British builders quote prices by the ton T.M. The defender was the *Puritan*, owned by a Boston Syndicate, headed by General Paine, a member of the New York Y.C., as well as the Eastern Y.C. This was the first time that Boston had defended the Cup, and it was a challenge which really should have succeeded.

The first race was postponed because of fog until 8th September 1885. On that day, when both boats were working towards the starting line, *Puritan* was hit fairly and squarely when she was on the port tack. She was immediately disqualified by the Committee, as she should have given way to the challenger, who was on the starboard tack. Sir Richard

Sutton then made a niche for himself in history, by refusing to sail over, and by asking for the race to be postponed until the damage to both boats was repaired. Such a contingency is now governed by the conditions agreed between the clubs concerned, but this display of sportsmanship surprised and delighted the Americans.

When the boats came out on 11th September there was such a light wind that the race was abandoned. When it was eventually started, on 14th September, *Genesta* was set to leeward of the line, and was then hampered by a big ship. However she picked up well, but was blanketed by the spectator fleet. Then the wind dropped away and the centre-board defender sailed away to win by 16 minutes on corrected time.

In the second race *Genesta* was ahead on the run to the mark, but carried too much sail for the beat home and was narrowly beaten. That ended the series and there was no doubt that she was the best yacht which had yet challenged. The accounts of the races seem to suggest that had she been sailed better she should have won. There is little excuse for being far from the starting line in any race, while there appears to have been an error of judgement in carrying too much sail in the second. It is, however, quite easy to be wise nearly a century later.

Galatea's challenge was postponed until the 1886 season. She had hardly won a race during 1885, so it was not surprising that the defender won easily. She was the *Mayflower*, another Burgess boat owned by General Paine. Although these two challenges were unsuccessful both Sir Richard Sutton and Lieutenant Henn were very popular and brought an air of good sportsmanship to the Cup races, which had sometimes been sadly lacking.

The next challenge was made by the Royal Clyde Y.C. with the cutter *Thistle*, designed by G. L. Watson. She was owned by a syndicate headed by the Vice-Commodore, James Bell, with Commodore John Clark, William Clark, Andrew

Coats, William Coats, James Coats, George Coats, J. Hilliard and William Bell.

In 1882, the Thames Tonnage rule: $\frac{L - B \times B \times \frac{1}{2}B,}{94}$ L, being length stem to sternpost on deck, and B, beam, was superseded by another rule which also penalized beam:

$$\frac{(LWL \times B)^2 \times B}{1730}$$

This in turn was replaced in 1886 by the famous length and sail area rule: $\frac{LWL \times SA}{6{,}000} = \text{Rating}$

This rule removed the penalty on beam so that *Thistle*, one of the first big boats to be built to it, was a comparatively beamy boat. There was great secrecy over her design and building and she won eleven of her first fifteen races. The Americans resented this secrecy, but it was mainly caused by a certain curtness in the New York Y.C.'s reply to the Royal Clyde's letter intimating that a challenge was about to be made.

To quote from *The Lawson History of the* America*'s Cup* (an American book): '*Thistle* arrived in this country on August 10th after a comfortable run of 22 days under short sail. The members of the syndicate came later in the steam yacht *Mohican*, owned by Robert Clark, arriving in New York on September 1st. They had bagpipers on board, a good supply of amber scotch liquor, some of which they declared they would drink from the *America*'s Cup. As the cup has no bottom to contain liquids the feat contemplated was as difficult as the task of winning the Cup itself.'

There was a fuss over *Thistle*'s measurement, as she was found to float on a waterline 1 foot 4 inches longer than the length stated in the challenge. The question whether she should be allowed to race was referred to Mr. George L. Schuyler, who, sensible as ever, ruled that the difference was automatically adjusted in the time allowance.

The obvious defender was *Volunteer*, a centreboard boat designed by Burgess for General Paine. Her keel had a certain amount of rocker, but not nearly as much as that of *Thistle*. Both had clipper bows.

The challenger was sailed by John Barr, elder brother of the great Charlie Barr, helmsman of many defenders. She was easily beaten in both her races, which was a great disappointment to Mr. Bell, who had a rope passed under her keel after the first race to see if she had fouled anything. He also expressed dissatisfaction with the New York Y.C. course, in which local knowledge paid very heavily. There was a rumour, proved to be baseless, that John Barr had been 'squared' to lose the races, but even so, it is difficult to find any reason why *Thistle* fared as badly as she did, in both light weather and a fresh breeze. Maybe a hint is given by the over-confident attitude of the owners when they first arrived in the U.S.A. *Thistle* was sold to the Kaiser and renamed *Meteor*, the first of his large racing yachts to bear that name.

In 1887 a new Deed of Gift was drawn up by Mr. Schuyler at the request of the New York Y.C. This clarified some points and increased the length of the notice required from the challenging club. It also required more information about the challenger, which was a direct result of the secrecy surrounding *Thistle*'s design.

The third Deed of Gift, which, with two modifications governs the contest today, reads as follows:

> This Deed of Gift, made October 24th, 1887, between George L. Schuyler, as sole surviving owner of the Cup won by the yacht *America* at Cowes, England, August 22nd, 1851, of the first part, and the New York Yacht Club, of the second part, witnesseth:
>
> That the said party of the first part, for and in consideration of the premises and the performance of the conditions and agreements hereinafter set forth by the party of the second part, has granted, bargained, sold, assigned, transferred and set over, and by these presents does bargain, sell, assign,

transfer and set over unto the said party of the second part, its successors and assigns, the Cup won by the schooner yacht *America* at Cowes, England, upon August 22nd, 1851, to have and to hold the same to the said party of the second part, its successors and assigns, in trust, nevertheless, for the following uses and purposes:

This Cup is donated upon the condition that it shall be preserved as a perpetual challenge Cup for friendly competition between foreign countries. Any organized yacht club of a foreign country, incorporated, patented or licensed by the Legislature, Admiralty or another executive department, having for its annual regatta an ocean water-course on the sea, or on an arm of the sea, or one which combines both, shall always be entitled to the right of sailing a match for this Cup with a yacht or vessel propelled by sails only and constructed in the country to which the challenging club belongs, against any one yacht or vessel constructed in the country of the club holding the Cup.

The yachts or vessels, if of one mast, shall be not less than sixty-five nor more than ninety feet on the load waterline: if of more than one mast, they shall be not less than eighty feet nor more than one hundred and fifteen feet on the load waterline.

The challenging club shall give ten months' notice in writing, naming the days for the proposed races, but no race shall be sailed on the days intervening between November 1st and May 1st. Accompanying the ten months' notice of challenge there must be sent the name of the owner and a certificate of the name, rig and following dimensions of the challenging vessel, namely: Length on load waterline, beam at load waterline, and extreme beam, and draft of water, which dimensions shall not be exceeded; and a Custom House registry of the vessel must be sent as soon as possible.

Vessels selected to compete for this Cup must proceed under sail on their own bottoms to the port where the contest is to take place.

Centreboard or sliding keel vessels shall always be allowed to compete in any race for this Cup, and no restriction or limitation whatever shall be placed upon the use of such centreboard or sliding keel, nor shall the centreboard or sliding keel be considered a part of the vessel for any purposes of measurement.

The club challenging for the Cup and the club holding the same may, by mutual consent, make any arrangement satisfactory to both as to the dates, courses, number of trials, rules, and sailing regulations, and any and all other conditions of the match, in which case, also, the ten months' notice may be waived.

In case the parties cannot mutually agree upon the terms of a match, then three races shall be sailed, and the winner of two of such races shall be entitled to the Cup. All such races shall be on ocean courses, free from headlands, as follows:

The first race, twenty nautical miles to windward and return; the second, an equilateral triangular race of thirty-nine nautical miles, the first side of which shall be a beat to windward; the third race, if necessary, twenty nautical miles to windward and return, and one week-day shall intervene between the conclusion of one race and the starting of the next race.

These ocean courses shall be practicable in all parts for vessels of twenty-two feet draft of water, and shall be selected by the club holding the Cup; and these races shall be sailed subject to its rules and sailing regulations, so far as the same do not conflict with the provisions of this Deed of Gift, but without any time allowance whatever.

The challenged club shall not be required to name its representative vessel until the time agreed upon for the start; but the vessel when named must compete in all the races, and each of such races must be completed within seven hours.

Should the club holding the Cup be, for any cause, dissolved, the Cup shall be transferred to some club of the same nationality eligible to challenge under this Deed of Gift, in trust and subject to its provisions. In the event of failure of such transfer within three months after such dissolution, said Cup shall revert to the preceding club holding the same, and under the terms of the Deed of Gift. It is distinctly understood that the Cup is to be the property of the club, subject to the provisions of this deed, and not the property of the owners of any vessel winning a match.

No vessel which has been defeated in a match for this Cup can be again selected by any club as its representative until after a contest for it by some other vessel has intervened, or until the expiration of two years from the time of such defeat. And when a challenge from a club fulfilling all the conditions required by this instrument has been received, no other challenge can be considered until the pending event has been decided.

And the said party of the second part hereby accepts the said Cup, subject to the said trust, terms, and conditions, and hereby covenants and agrees, to and with the said party of the first part, that it will faithfully and fully see that the foregoing conditions are fully observed and complied with by any contestant for the said Cup during the holding thereof by it, and that it will assign, transfer, and deliver the said Cup to the foreign yacht club whose representative yacht shall have won the same in accordance with the foregoing terms and conditions, provided that the said foreign club shall, by instrument in writing, lawfully executed, enter into the like covenants as are herein entered into by it, such instrument to contain a like provision for the successive assignees to enter into the same covenants with their respective assignors, and to be executed in duplicate, one to be retained by each club, and a copy thereof forwarded to the party of the second part.

In witness whereof said party of the first part has hereunto set his hand and seal, and the said party of the second part has caused its corporate seal to be affixed to these presents, and the same to be signed by its commodore and attested by its secretary, the day and year first above written.

GEORGE L. SCHUYLER
THE NEW YORK YACHT CLUB
BY ELBRIDGE T. GERRY
Commodore
JOHN H. BIRD
Secretary

It is said that the legal tone of this document caused it to be treated with suspicion by foreign clubs, many regarding it as unfair. More important was the clause requiring the challenger to give the length on load waterline ten months in advance, which has virtually been the cause of challenges being made with vessels which have not even floated. It was this clause which made Mr. Bell ask the Royal Clyde to withdraw the challenge which they had made on his behalf. However, the New York Y.C. course was no longer to be used, which stopped any suggestion that the races were to be won by local knowledge.

Another challenge, in 1889, by the Royal Yacht Squadron, naming a vessel called *Valkyrie*, owned by the Earl of Dunraven, also fell through. This gave the waterline as not exceeding 70 feet, but the Squadron refused to hold the Cup on the terms of the Deed of Gift, if they won it, because they considered it unfair.

Sadly enough Mr. Schuyler died before another contest was decided. He had done much to ease matters, which were not always handled without bias by the New York Y.C., by giving commonsense rulings when acrimony threatened to produce deadlock.

II

1893 to 1920—The Valkyries *and* Shamrocks

A NEW challenge was made at the end of 1892 naming *Valkyrie II*, also owned by the Earl of Dunraven and designed by George L. Watson. She was a very near sister to the famous Royal Cutter *Britannia*, which was built in the next berth at Henderson's, Glasgow. The New York Y.C. agreed to accept the waterline length as the only measurement required, with a penalty if it was exceeded. The Royal Yacht Squadron in turn agreed, if they won, to accept any future challenge under the terms of the 1887 Deed, on the same conditions which applied to *Valkyrie*'s challenge. The series was to consist of the best of five races and the challenger was to be eighty-five feet along the waterline.

The defender was *Vigilant*, owned by a syndicate led by C. Oliver Iselin, and designed by Nathaniel G. Herreshoff. She was very nearly a fin keeler, following a famous Herreshoff boat called *Gloriana*, and she had a centreboard.

The first race was sailed on 5th October, but was abandoned due to lack of wind, after the challenger had reached the outer mark 26 minutes ahead. The next day *Vigilant* won by over seven minutes, the challenger having shown a good turn of speed on the leg home, on which both boats could easily lay the line.

The second race was in a fairly hard wind. *Vigilant* got the start, led by nearly five minutes at the weather mark, increasing this to ten minutes after two reaches to the finish. There was a strong wind for the next and last race, on 13th

October, which must have been one of the most magnificent in the whole history of the Cup. It blew so hard that the designer took charge of the defender, whose professional skipper did not like the look of the weather. *Valkyrie* outsailed her on the beat to the weather mark, leading there by nearly two minutes. Unfortunately her spinnaker, which was set flying (modern sailing crews may be surprised to hear that this was current British fashion), tore slightly on the bitts while being hoisted. It finished in ribbons. The light weather one was set in its place, but did not last long. As a last resort a balloon jib-topsail was set as a spinnaker. The reefs in the mainsail were not shaken out, nor was a larger topsail set above it.

Meanwhile the crew of seventy men in *Vigilant* (*Valkyrie* had thirty-five) were working like beavers. They set the spinnaker, shook out the reefs in the main and hoisted it right up. They also set a small jackyarder in place of the working topsail. It all sounds easy, but in half a gale it must have been a superb feat of seamanship. She caught and passed *Valkyrie* to beat her by 40 seconds on corrected time.

Clinton Crane, in his memoirs, records that Nat Herreshoff judged that *Valkyrie II* was a better boat than the defender. *Vigilant*'s sail area was 11,272 square feet compared with 10,042 set by the challenger.

Valkyrie returned to this country the following spring and was sunk in collision with *Satanita*, off Hunter's Quay, in almost the first race of the 1894 season. *Vigilant* followed her across the Atlantic, but met with little success, her chief opponent was the Prince of Wales's *Britannia*, which won twelve against *Vigilant*'s five of their encounters.

Maybe *Valkyrie II* would have fared better in the States if weather conditions had been right. It was also a pity about those spinnakers in the last race, but there seems little doubt that the defender thoroughly deserved to win it.

The Squadron challenged again in 1894 for a series in the autumn of 1895. The challenger was to be eighty-nine feet along the waterline and G. L. Watson designed a boat very much on the American model. Owned by Lord Dunraven in partnership with Lord Lonsdale, Lord Wolverton, and Captain Harry McCalmont, she was the first of the pure racing machines to challenge, and carried 13,028 square feet of sail. She was not a success in England, only beating *Britannia* once out of three races.

Herreshoff designed the appropriately named *Defender*, owned by C. Oliver Iselin, W. K. Vanderbilt, and E. D. Morgan. He had obviously been impressed enough by *Valkyrie II* to make his new boat more of an English model with easy bilges. It paid in the first race, which she won on 7th September 1895, particularly when the wind freshened and there was quite a lop.

At the end of this race Lord Dunraven wrote to the New York Y.C. complaining that *Valkyrie III* had been hampered by the pleasure fleet, which was justifiable and which the New York Y.C. promised to try to rectify. He also complained that *Defender* had been seen taking in ballast during the night. Both yachts were measured, showing differences of $\frac{1}{8}$ and $\frac{1}{16}$ of an inch, respectively, so it appears that the charge was unfounded.

Valkyrie III was disqualified for fouling *Defender* at the start of the next race, breaking her topmast stay. Both boats had again been hampered by the spectator fleet and a large steamer separated them just before the start. *Valkyrie* did not stop, nor did her skipper make any attempt to find out the extent of the damage to *Defender*, whom she actually beat by 47 seconds. Mr. Iselin wrote to Lord Dunraven offering to resail the race, but this the latter refused, as the matter was at an end as far as he was concerned.

Lord Dunraven then complained again of the spectator fleet, and the Cup committee agreed not to start the next race until there was a clear enough space to allow the boats to manœuvre. They stated, however, that they could not guarantee to keep the rest of the course clear, as they could not control sightseers. Lord Dunraven then wrote once more, agreeing to sail the race on the condition that the Committee would declare the race void if either vessel was interfered with by 'steamers and tugboats'. He also said, that if the Committee did not agree, he would cross the starting line, to give *Defender* a start, and immediately retire. Unfortunately the Committee did not receive this until the morning of the race, when it was too late.

Valkyrie appeared on the starting line, crossed it with *Defender*, although she still had her topsails in stops. As soon as the challenger was clear of the line she luffed sharply, hauled down her racing flag, hoisted the burgee of the New York Y.C., of which Lord Dunraven was an Honorary Member, and returned to her moorings.

There was quite a lot of bitterness about this incident alone, but much worse was to follow. Lord Dunraven returned home and in an article in *The Field* of 9th November he repeated his charges concerning the shifting of ballast. He followed this with a speech, on 21st November, which was widely reported. Quite rightly Mr. Iselin asked the New York Y.C. for an inquiry.

Lord Dunraven took his lawyer to this and repeated his charges. It was clearly established, however, that on the night in question twenty-one pigs of ballast, which were too big to be stowed properly, were taken from *Defender*, cut in half aboard her tender and then replaced. This was the 'taking in' of ballast of which he had complained. The report of the Committee was so worded as to give his Lordship a chance to withdraw and tender an apology to close the matter. After a month no such apology had been received, so the club asked for his resignation as an Honorary Member. This was ignored, although Lord Dunraven maintained that he had already resigned, so he was expelled. Thus ended a rather unsavoury incident, which might have been avoided if the defenders had given notice of their intention to remove the ballast during the night and to replace it.

Before the article appeared in *The Field*, the Royal Victoria Y.C. challenged with a yacht called *Distant Shore*, owned by Mr. C. D. Rose, but this was withdrawn and never renewed.

After the Dunraven trouble few thought that there would be another challenge, at least for several years. But, in the autumn of 1898, the New York Y.C. received a cable from the Royal Ulster Y.C. giving notice of their intention to do so with a yacht owned by Sir Thomas Lipton. Well known even to this day as an astonishingly successful grocer, Sir Thomas was a friend of King Edward VII, then Prince of Wales. It is said that although Lipton always had taken a great interest in the Cup races, it was actually at the suggestion of the Prince of Wales that he challenged when he did. The latter had hoped that his friend's endearing personality would remove the bitterness which still lingered.

These hopes were fulfilled. Lipton was a great sportsman and relations between the New York Y.C. and the challengers were elevated to the plane of 'friendly competition' once more. At times they did have slight qualms over the frequent suggestions that they were being used to help the sale of Lipton's wares, but at least the wrangling over the cup races was stopped.

The first *Shamrock* was designed by William Fife, the third of the famous Fifes of Fairlie. He had the reputation of being a great autocrat, who built some of the most beautiful vessels of his day, but seldom allowed an owner near his yard until his boat was ready. He visited the U.S.A. with the Royal Ulster delegation, which went to fix up the details of the match. His new challenger was designed to follow the general shape of light displacement yachts encouraged by the current American measurement rules. *Shamrock I* was built by Thornycroft's at Millwall. A suggestion by Sir Thomas that she should be built in his beloved Ireland, at Harland and Wolff's, Belfast, was turned down by the chairman of that firm. She was a big boat, 128 feet overall, 89 feet 8 inches W.L., carrying 13,492 square feet of sail. Her bottom was manganese bronze, topsides aluminium and she was specially strengthened for the Atlantic crossing.

The defender was *Columbia*, owned by a syndicate led by J. Pierpont Morgan and C. Oliver Iselin, under the management of the latter. She was designed and built by Nat Herreshoff and skippered by Charlie Barr, a Scotsman by birth, but by then an American citizen. An outcry about this in the American press was sensibly ignored by Mr. Iselin, because Barr must rank as one of the very greatest racing skippers of all time.

Shamrock was towed most of the way across the Atlantic, provision being made for this under the mutual agreement clause in the Deed of Gift.

Unexpectedly light conditions prevailed when the series started, on 3rd October 1899, the first race not being completed until the 16th. The spectator fleet was even bigger than that which was watching *Valkyrie III*'s races, but for this, and all challenges since, the course was patrolled by the U.S. Navy, or Coastguards.

Shamrock broke her topmast in the second race, the defender having won the first quite easily, as she also did the third. According to an authority of those days, *Shamrock* was never in proper trim. This may have been due to the illness which prevented Fife from supervising her tuning up, on the other side of the Atlantic.

Sir Thomas Lipton waited all the summer of 1900 to see if anyone else would challenge. As no one was interested, he asked the Royal Ulster to do so again, on 2nd October. The waterline length of *Shamrock II* was given as ninety feet and her designer was George L. Watson, who had been responsible for *Thistle* and the *Valkyries*.

Watson conducted a series of tank tests at Denny's of Dumbarton, with models at various angles of keel. There is no doubt that the result was a very fast boat. She was a more extreme type than the first *Shamrock*, but even so there was quite a noticeable resemblance to the *Valkyrie II* and *Britannia* model. On her early trials she was found not to be as fast as her predecessor, but she improved as the season progressed. She was dismasted off Cowes, with King Edward VII and some ladies on board, during a trial race. As the mast was being cut away, a Scottish voice was heard by Charles Nicholson above the noise of the wind and waves: 'Charlie, Charlie, what did I tell ye. A racing yacht's no place for a King and his harlots!'

Sir Thomas was given a month's delay for the cup races by the New York Y.C., and oddly enough the new possible defender, *Constitution*, also lost her mast. She never sailed as well as *Columbia*. Another possible defender entered the field. She was called *Independence* and was owned by Thomas Lawson, of Boston, who was not a member of the New York Y.C. The latter told him that he would either have to join, or charter his boat to a member, if he wished to defend the Cup. He refused, but as his boat was the slowest of the three, she never had a chance anyway. It was this gentleman who commissioned the writing of the very entertaining history of the Cup, which bears his name.

Columbia was selected to defend once more, giving the challenger an excellent chance. Mr. Iselin had sold his share in her to E. D. Morgan, but she was still sailed by Charlie Barr. Captain Sycamore took the helm of the challenger. The races started on the 28th September 1901, the first attempt two days before having been abandoned, due to light weather, with *Columbia* well ahead. They were really very close, with the defender winning each. The reasons for the challenger's defeat were stated by *British Yachts and Yachtsmen* to have been lack of careful tuning up at home, and inferior handling. As with *Valkyrie II*, Nat Herreshoff is said to have judged that George Watson's second challenger was a better boat than his defender.

Sir Thomas was naturally disappointed at not winning but

waited for the summer to end before asking the Royal Ulster to challenge again. The new challenger was designed by William Fife, and built by Denny's, at Dumbarton. She was outbuilt. Herreshoff produced the most astonishing defender called *Reliance.* She was owned by a syndicate of the New York Y.C. millionaires consisting of William Rockefeller, Cornelius Vanderbilt, P. A. B. Widener, Henry Walters, W. B. Leeds, Elbert H. Gary, Clement A. Griscan, Norman Ream, and James J. Hill. Oliver Iselin was once again the manager, with Charlie Barr at the helm.

Reliance was designed to heel to her lee rail in a breeze of eight knots. She had 16,160 square feet of sail, about 1,800 more than the challenger, and had a socketed topmast and a lot of winches which were an innovation. In spite of *Shamrock III* having *Shamrock I* to tune her up she never had a hope.

The series started, as seemed common, with an abortive race on 20th August, which was followed by a proper one on 22nd August, which the defender won easily. *Shamrock*'s mainsail set badly, but was better in the next race, won again by the defender by a smaller margin, mainly because she ran into a flat spot. *Shamrock* never finished the last race, faulty navigation taking her well clear of the finishing line in the fog, when the defender had already crossed it. And so the cup remained in the New York Y.C.

It was quite obvious that by now the cup races were producing a type of vessel which was quite useless for anything else; a ridiculously extravagant state of affairs. The defender only had to be strong enough to last the season, while the challenger had to cross the Atlantic. As the measurement rules were different on each side of the Atlantic there was little use for the challenger when her mission was completed, except as a pacemaker for her successors.

In the early years of the twentieth century, the Americans adopted the Universal Rule, while a little later, in 1907 the so-called International Rule was adopted in Europe. Both produced a more healthy type of boat than had been encouraged by the previous rating rules, which had ignored displacement. Uffa Fox in his book shows how similar *Shamrock III*'s midship section was to the Scandinavian Skerry cruisers, which were popular between the wars, but really only in the waters for which they were intended.

Sir Thomas tried to make the New York Y.C. agree to bind the contestants to the Universal Rule, but they refused. He even issued a challenge in 1907, conditional on the yachts being built to it, with the defender no longer on the waterline than the challenger, but this was turned down. He tried again in 1912, suggesting a yacht of seventy-five feet waterline, provided the New York Y.C. would defend with a similar vessel, but this was again refused. He then issued an unconditional challenge in 1913, which was immediately accepted. After this the Club agreed under the mutual agreement clause in the Deed of Gift, to build the defender to the Universal Rule, but they reserved the right to decide the waterline length.

Shamrock IV was designed by Charles E. Nicholson, who had studied the Universal Rule, but observers at the time of her appearance remarked on the obvious influence of the 'length and sail area rule' to which most racing boats in England had been built for many years. She had a very pronounced tumble home, which Nicholson usually put on his boats. She was very round forward, which had the effect of stopping her in a head sea, in certain conditions. She was the first British challenger to have a centreboard, and had a socketed topmast, similar to *Reliance*. Her construction plan was very advanced, and she even had a plywood deck, the ply being made in Russia.

In America there were three possible defenders, *Vanitie*, *Defiance*, and *Resolute*. The latter was the best, designed and built by Herreshoff, the 'Wizard of Bristol', and owned by a syndicate headed by Cornelius Vanderbilt.

Shamrock was in mid-Atlantic when the war started and was laid up at Brooklyn on arrival in U.S.A. She was not very well looked after during the war, and it was not until 1920 that arrangements were made to refit her for the races, which had been arranged to start on 20th July. Sir Thomas fitted out the twenty-three-metre *Shamrock*, not one of the cup challengers, to act as trial horse and a description of her voyage, the trials and the cup races can be found in the log of Tom Diaper, who was her mate.

Resolute was chosen as the defender. She was about the same waterline length as the challenger (seventy-five feet), but was shorter overall, with only 8,775 square feet of sail compared with 9,860. She was allowed 7 minutes 1 second by her, although the time allowance was not announced until the morning of the first race. *Shamrock* appeared that morning with a canvas fairing sleeve round the mast but this was only used for that race as the Committee threatened to measure it as part of the sail area. She was over the line at the start, but did not lose much by it.

Her helmsman was W. P. Burton, with Mrs. Burton, Charles E. Nicholson, Duncan Neill (Lipton's adviser), and Captain Turner as the afterguard. Sherman Hoyt was the New York Y.C. observer. He remarked in his memoirs on the continual arguments which went on between Burton, Nicholson, Neill, and Turner and of the resentment shown by some members of the crew to the presence on board of Mrs. Burton. Mr. Burton, later Sir William, was one of the finest helmsmen of his day, but there was quite a lot of criticism of his selection, being the first amateur to steer a challenger.

Resolute, sailed by Charles Francis Adams, was in trouble, just before she reached the mark, as her throat halyard had gone. At the same time *Shamrock* was also in trouble, but was sailed 'easy'. *Resolute* then withdrew leaving her to sail home to win the first race to be won by a challenger since *Livonia*, in 1871. That victory was also due to damage to the defender.

After an abortive attempt to race on the 17th, *Shamrock* sailed well to win on the 20th. Nicholson had stayed ashore that day, his place being taken by a Sandy Hook pilot. Sherman Hoyt, in his memoirs, remarks on uncertainty in locating marks and windshifts. Her topmast was also shaky and although renewed later, remained a constant worry.

Nicholson rejoined for the third race and there were apparently fewer arguments. Burton, Nicholson, and Turner all took turns at the wheel to windward. *Resolute* was a couple of minutes ahead at the mark, but *Shamrock* passed her on the run home leading her over the line by a few seconds, but losing the race on corrected time. The defender won the fourth race quite easily to square the series, but it took three attempts to finish it. At the first there was too much wind, at the second too little even to get to the first mark.

On the 27th July *Shamrock* was fairly and squarely beaten, getting the worst of the windshifts, in spite of some beautiful windward sailing by Nicholson.

One of the features of *Resolute* was the vang, which held her gaff nearer amidships than it would normally lie, and so helped her to point higher on the wind than *Shamrock*. More than one writer has remarked that there were too many experts in the afterguard of the challenger, and this may well have been so. It tends to be a common English fault.

This series ended one phase of the cup races. No longer were they to be held in gaff rigged yachts racing on time allowance. Never again were the boats built without any scantling regulations. Of the eleven British challengers, four, *Genesta*, *Valkyrie II*, *Shamrock II*, and *Shamrock IV*, at least showed that they had a chance of winning, but one or other of the many factors which go to help success in a racing yacht were lacking. Perhaps most important of all was consideration of the human element.

III

1930 to 1937—Rainbow *and the* Endeavours

IT was not until May 1929 that a new challenge, by the Royal Ulster Y.C., was made and accepted. The yacht was Sir Thomas Lipton's fifth *Shamrock*. After the first war there was a gradual movement towards agreement between America and Europe on the rules for measurement and construction of yachts. As already mentioned, the Americans had adopted the Universal Rule, while the countries affiliated to the International Yacht Racing Union (mostly in Europe) had adopted the so-called International Rule. Full agreement was eventually reached in 1931 to use the latter for yachts of less than fourteen and a half metres rating, and the Universal Rule for those above.

The new challenger was built to the Universal 'J' class rule. The rating of a 'J' class yacht was found as follows: Eighteen per cent of the waterline length in feet, multiplied by the square root of the sail area (in square feet) divided by the cube root of the displacement (in cubic feet). The waterline length could vary from seventy to eighty-seven feet, while the rating was always seventy-six feet. As can be seen by this formula, the rating was increased by increasing the waterline length, and decreased by increasing displacement. Roughly the bigger the waterline, the bigger the displacement, but these generally offset each other so that the measured sail area of a 'J' boat was always within a few square feet of 7,550.

The Americans built four possible defenders, *Yankee*, *Weetamoe*, *Whirlwind*, and *Enterprise*. After trials in August

1930, the latter was chosen. She was designed by Starling Burgess and sailed by H. S. Vanderbilt, one of the New York Y.C. syndicate who owned her.

Both challenger and defender were built, as required by the 'J' class rule, to the scantling requirements of Lloyd's Register of Shipping, so that there could be no question of rapid deterioration after the races, or of the defender being built more lightly. *Shamrock V* is still to be seen in the Mediterranean rigged as a ketch. She was designed by Charles E. Nicholson and built by Camper and Nicholson's at their Gosport yard. She had a successful first season in this country, racing against *Cambria* and *Candida.* She and the defender were both Bermuda rigged and many writers of that time were optimistic as to her chance. Her helmsman was Ned Heard, the last professional to steer a cup challenger. A friend who had sailed in *Enterprise* during the defender's trials was not impressed on her arrival in U.S.A.

'You couldn't help wondering whether she had come by mistake,' he remarked.

Enterprise was astonishing. The Americans at that time had suddenly leapt ahead with improvements to gear, rigging, masts and sails, on which they had carried out many tests. Her mast was duralumin, costing £8,000, weighing only 4,000 lbs compared with 6,200 lbs of *Shamrock*'s wooden stick. She also had a 'Park Avenue' boom, triangular in section, on which there were transverse slides attached to the foot of the sail. The flow of the sail could be adjusted along the boom, increased in light weather and decreased in heavy, by stops in these tracks. The flat top to the boom also stopped the downward escape of wind from the mainsail. She had a lot of very efficient winches, some of which were operated entirely from down below, the interior being completely clear of any accommodation. She cost £150,000 compared with the £30,000 for the challenger.

The series was to consist of the best of seven races with no time allowance. The first started on 13th September with a run to the mark in a northerly breeze. It was on this run that *Enterprise* set a small spinnaker and tacked to leeward, in doing so she sailed away from the challenger, which had steered straight towards the mark, but the defender's crew did not see it until it was nearly broad on the beam. *Shamrock* was thus able to reduce the lead slightly, which shows the absolute necessity for accurate navigation in these races. *Enterprise* was 1 minute 54 seconds ahead at the mark and gained nearly another minute on the close fetch home, in spite of being forced by a windshift to make two short tacks to the finishing line, which *Shamrock* made without tacking. This gave some idea of the defender's potential speed to windward.

It was demonstrated again on 15th September in a light south-westerly. On the beat to the first mark *Enterprise* led by six minutes. She gained another three and a half on the two reaches to win by 9 minutes 34 seconds.

Fog caused postponement of the third race until 17th September. *Shamrock* got the better start, but before long *Enterprise* was ahead. After about three-quarters of an hour the challenger's main halyard parted, her mainsail fell down, which left the defender to finish alone.

The last race was sailed on the 18th, over the triangular course. The defender had the better of the start and sailed away on the beat to lead by just over nine minutes at the first mark. *Shamrock* sailed well on the reaches, but could not catch her rival, which won by 5 minutes 44 seconds, her elapsed time of 3 hours 10 minutes and 13 seconds being a new record for the triangular course, 3 minutes 5 seconds better than that set up by *Columbia* in 1901.

Many have remarked that as far as hull form was concerned there was little difference between the two contestants, which was of credit to Nicholson in his first attempt at a 'J' boat. There was no doubt, however, that the absence of cabin fittings and her superiority aloft made a big difference to the defender's performance, particularly to windward.

Sir Thomas Lipton was getting very old and he died in 1931, aged eighty-two, having been elected a member of the Royal Yacht Squadron in May of that year. At the time of his death he was planning a sixth attempt to win the 'Old Mug' which had undoubtedly become his life's ambition, and on which he had spent a fortune. It has been suggested that his yachting manager, Duncan Neill, was never really given the 'blank cheque' that is so necessary if the challenger is to be as well equipped as the defender.

In 1932 *Shamrock V* was the most successful of the 'J' class. She had been bought by Mr. T. O. M. (now Sir Thomas) Sopwith, who had been very successful with the twelve metre *Mouette*, and who was a very good amateur helmsman. In 1933 a challenge was sent on his behalf by the Royal Yacht Squadron, naming a new 'J' boat, *Endeavour*. She was designed by Charles E. Nicholson and built at his yard at Gosport.

As can be seen from the table of dimensions of the 'J' class challengers and defenders, on page 41, she was not up to the length limit of that class. She was a very successful boat from the start, winning her first race and many others in the 1934 season. She had a Park Avenue boom and a tubular steel mast, but perhaps one of her most interesting features was the very efficient quadrilateral jib, which combined jib and jib topsail. This had been evolved by Sopwith, but unfortunately it was spotted by Sherman Hoyt, who was out sailing and watching a race off Ryde between *Endeavour* and *Velsheda*. It was therefore copied by the defender, and later exploited to the full by H. S. Vanderbilt in *Ranger* in 1937.

On the eve of her departure for the U.S.A. most of the professional crew of *Endeavour* struck for higher wages. Sopwith asked the Commodore of the Royal Corinthian Y.C. to fill the vacancies with amateur volunteers, who were found within a few hours. These men were: Allen Bacon, James Bacon, M. A. Belville, C. A. Boardman, W. de Quincey, Reginald Droop, David Kemsley, Jake Martin, J. F. R.

Mitchell, Beecher Moore, Colin Ratsey, Dr. W. F. Richards, and Nigel Warington-Smyth, some of whom are leaders of the sport at the present time. Although not as good as the professionals they replaced, they enabled the challenger to sail for America on the day originally planned.

The defender was *Rainbow*, sailed by H. S. Vanderbilt, one of the owning syndicate, which had just won the trials sailed with *Yankee*, *Weetamoe* having been eliminated. She had a duralumin mast, as in *Enterprise*, which was of a greater section than *Endeavour*'s steel one. Instead of the Park Avenue boom, hers was fitted with struts and winches and could be bent to the flow of the sail. Her sheet winches were on deck, unlike those in *Enterprise*, but her cabin fittings were pretty sparse, two of the seven tons required consisting of batteries under the cabin floor! Sopwith was allowed to remove such fittings as he liked if he thought there was inequality, but there was hardly time to do this properly.

The races were held off Brenton Reef Light Vessel, but the first on 15th September was abandoned, with *Rainbow* becalmed within a mile of the finish, about a mile ahead of *Endeavour*. There was a good breeze on the following Monday, 17th September. The start was postponed fifteen minutes to allow *Endeavour* to hoist her mainsail, with which there had been trouble in the swell. Many Americans commented on the illegality of this action by the race committee. *Endeavour* was slightly ahead and to leeward of *Rainbow*, but before long the latter was in the lead. It was when *Rainbow* tacked for the mark that Vanderbilt noticed how fast *Endeavour* was. She had overstood by a couple of minutes and Sopwith then drove her hard for the mark with what is known as 'a good full'. This astonished Vanderbilt as the challenger only rounded 18 seconds astern. *Endeavour*'s spinnaker was not broken out until three minutes after the defender's, but once it was drawing she gained, passing *Rainbow* to win by 2 minutes 9 seconds.

There was another good breeze for the second race, the

next day. The start for the triangular course was on a reach and Sopwith was first over the line, sailing through *Rainbow*'s lee. The latter dropped back into the challenger's wake about a length astern and got a tow from her, remaining in exactly the same position for about eight miles. *Endeavour* sailed a little faster on the beat and gained again when both boats overstood the mark. The defender reduced this on the reach home because *Endeavour* had torn her genoa at the start and had to use a balloon jib. Even so she won by 51 seconds, in record time, and was two up.

The next race was postponed until 20th September. Sopwith had the windward berth at the start and *Endeavour* ran away, rounding the mark 6 minutes ahead, *Rainbow* having had constant trouble with her spinnaker. On rounding both boats found that they could lay the finishing line, but the wind fell light. Vanderbilt handed the wheel of *Rainbow* to Sherman Hoyt, as he often did in such conditions. The latter abandoned all attempt to sail the normal course home, luffed as high as he could to get way on the boat. This and the fact that *Endeavour*'s genoa was a very poor baggy sail lent by Gerard Lambert, the owner of *Vanitie*, led Sopwith into making a fatal tack over towards *Rainbow* and away from the finishing line, an astonishing thing to do with nearly ten miles to go. *Endeavour* crossed *Rainbow* by a bare three lengths and tacked too late to cover her. Hoyt pinched up to leebow Sopwith who was forced to tack again to clear his wind. He then had to tack once more in the direction of the finish, which he had always been able to lay, and which *Rainbow* made without tacking to win by 3 minutes 25 seconds.

Sir Thomas Sopwith has been much criticized for this tactical error, which undoubtedly cost him the race and probably the Cup. It was a brilliant piece of helmsmanship by Sherman Hoyt, who knew from experience in England of Sopwith's tendency to cover his opponent at all costs, regardless of the true course to the finish.

There was then a rest day. *Endeavour* had removed and *Rainbow* had shipped some ballast, before the third race, which seemed to improve the latter, which was not as stiff as the challenger. Vanderbilt was worried about the defender's downwind performance. Her spinnaker was invariably up before *Endeavour's*, but once the latter's was drawing (it was usually a better sail), she ran much faster. Vanderbilt therefore asked Frank C. Paine, designer of *Yankee*, to come and take charge of his spinnaker department. This he did, bringing *Yankee's* parachute spinnaker with him.

The fourth race started in a moderate breeze, and was spoilt by two protests, which were never heard. The first incident occurred just before the start. Both boats reached away from the line on the starboard tack with *Endeavour* ahead of *Rainbow*. The former bore away in a wide circle and gybed to come on the wind. The latter bore away well inside *Endeavour's* track and, cutting the corner, sailed to leeward with her boom to port (starboard tack), until she met *Endeavour* reaching along on the port tack. [Diagram 1.] Both boats had to alter course to avoid a collision and as a result *Rainbow* was well ahead, on the first leg of the triangle. She was caught by *Endeavour* because once again the challenger had overstood and gained by being driven for the mark, racing towards it with 'a good full'. There was then the luff by *Endeavour*, as *Rainbow* passed through her weather, to which *Rainbow* did not respond, which led to the second protest. Those on board *Rainbow*, except Sherman Hoyt, maintained that *Endeavour* would not have hit her forward of the shrouds, had she not borne away. The defender went on to win by a minute and a quarter.

Sir Thomas Sopwith recalls that the two boats were so close that he had to be careful not to hit *Rainbow* with *Endeavour's* counter as she bore away.

On the advice of the New York Y.C. observer on board *Endeavour* Mr. Sopwith did not immediately hoist a protest flag, but waited until *Endeavour* was approaching the finish.

Sir Richard Sutton's Genesta *racing against* Ilex, *in the Solent*

The Earl of Dunraven's Valkyrie II

Sir Thomas Sopwith's two challengers, Endeavour II *(left) and* Endeavour I

H. S. Vanderbilt's Ranger *winning the last race of the* 1937 America*'s Cup series*

H. S. Vanderbilt's Vim, *the most successful Twelve Metre in British waters in* 1939

Much valuable practice was obtained in Owen Aisher's Evaine, 1957

American Twelve Metres, Gleam, Nyala, *and* Vim, *practising in Long Island Sound,* 1957

The nine tank test models

The yacht model here is in the small docking bay at one end of the tank. The dynamometer, top centre, is being adjusted by Norman Bromfield

The model is heeling over under conditions representing high wind speed

Mr. Boyd (top left) in conversation with plumber Gerry Simmons during the casting of the keel

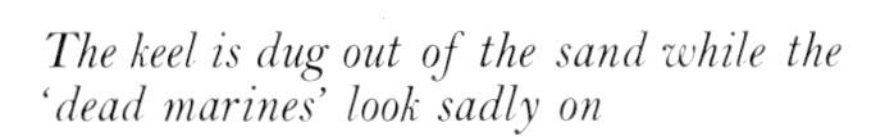

The keel is dug out of the sand while the 'dead marines' look sadly on

The wood and lead keels are bolted together, and the first frame is put in place

ith the steel frames in place, the hull form emerges

View under the counter, showing plank ing almost completed

Looking aft, showing the wood and steel structure

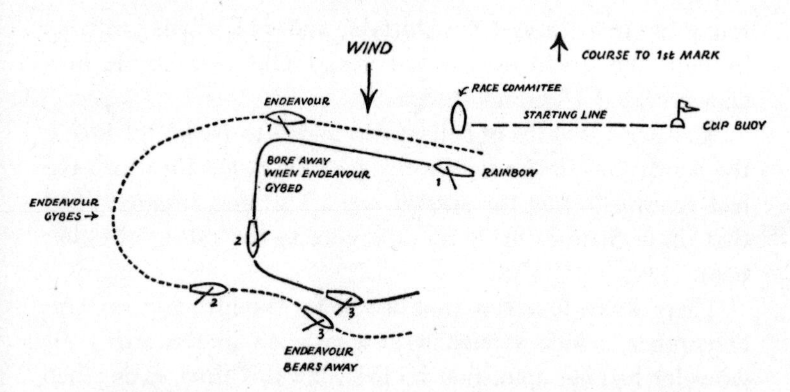

Was *Rainbow* still the overtaking yacht when, having held away before the wind, and still on the starboard tack, she met *Endeavour* approaching at right angles after *Endeavour* had gybed onto port? If *Rainbow* was still overtaking she was in the wrong, otherwise she was right.

Diagram 1

The Race Committee refused to hear the protests because the flag was not hoisted 'promptly', as required by the New York Y.C. racing rules, which governed the races. Opinions differ as to what the result would have been. The full stories are told in Vanderbilt's *On the Wind's Highway* and in *Further Memorials of the Royal Yacht Squadron*, for the benefit of sea lawyers who want to judge for themselves. It seems quite possible that the Committee, who had watched the first incident, might have disqualified *Endeavour*, so that the merits of the second case would have been purely academic.

Many felt quite sincerely that Sopwith had been shabbily treated. The refusal to hear the protest almost certainly had a psychological effect on him and his crew in the next race. However, one result of the furore was a close study of the overtaking rules, particularly by Vanderbilt. He introduced a new code of racing rules which are the basis of those used today in America and Scandinavia, and which will probably be used the world over before long. This remarkable man also invented Contract Bridge.

Another 1,000 lbs of ballast was added to *Rainbow*, during the Sunday, while *Endeavour* replaced the 3,360 lbs which she had removed after the second race. The measurer certified that these changes made no difference to the rating of either boat.

There was a fourteen-knot breeze for the fifth race on 24th September, which started with a run. As in the third, the defender had her spinnaker up first, but this time, even when *Endeavour* had hers set, *Rainbow* gained steadily. In spite of tearing the spinnaker and knocking a man overboard, who was miraculously recovered, the defender went on to win by 4 minutes 1 second, *Endeavour*'s only decisive defeat of the series.

There was a broad reach to the first mark of the triangular course in the sixth race on the 26th September. Protest flags were hoisted by both boats at the start, but both protests were withdrawn on return to port. The situation causing the trouble had been almost the same as at the start of the fourth race. This time instead of gybing, *Rainbow* luffed and passed astern of *Endeavour* to avoid a collision and the latter did not have to alter. Vanderbilt considers that Sopwith only hoisted a protest flag to protect his rights. The consequence of these manœuvres was that *Endeavour* won the start, being well ahead. *Rainbow* caught up, but only after being luffed head to wind by *Endeavour*. It was this encounter which caused Vanderbilt to remark how quickly *Endeavour* gathered way, leaving her 'as though she were an "M" boat'. He suggests that it may have been due to her painted bottom, compared to *Rainbow*'s bronze, or her lines, or 'a combination of other factors'.

On the beat the challenger lost through holding on to her genoa, after rounding 1 minute 19 seconds ahead. Sopwith and his crew had not had much experience of these sails and it was a mistake to carry it in that weight of wind. Consequently she had to let *Rainbow* go off on her own, while she changed to working headsails rather slowly. This and a wind-shift put *Rainbow* ahead. The latter broke out the wrong spinnaker by mistake on the run to the line, but *Endeavour* did not have hers drawing until 7 minutes after she rounded the mark.

She started to gain rapidly so that the defender's lead of four hundred yards was soon cut to a couple of lengths, with *Endeavour* out on *Rainbow*'s weather beam.

It was here that Sherman Hoyt took over the helm at another critical time. Again he gambled on Sopwith's tendency to try to keep an opponent covered, regardless of course. He asked the navigator, Zenas Bliss, to give him a course to a point one mile to leeward of the finishing line, then only five miles away. He bore away on it, and Sopwith followed in an attempt to take *Rainbow*'s wind. As a result both boats were running 'by-the-lee', with the challenger even more so than the defender, instead of heading straight for the finish. About a mile from the line Hoyt luffed on to the proper course for it. Being slightly to leeward with the wind on her quarter *Rainbow* pulled ahead to win by 55 seconds. The Cup was once more safe on its pedestal in the New York Y.C., but only just.

Vanderbilt in his book *On the Wind's Highway* considered that errors played the major part in this successful defence. *Endeavour* was a faster boat than either *Rainbow* or *Yankee*. The former was not ballasted down enough, nor until Frank Paine joined were her spinnakers good enough. In turn *Endeavour* was handicapped by the inexperience of her crew, lack of familiarity with genoas, and by a perhaps fatal tactical error in the third race.

It was all very sad, most of all to Mr. Sopwith, his crew and to Charles E. Nicholson, who had produced a magnificent boat. A lot of bitterness remained as a result of the refusal to hear the protests in the fourth race. Sopwith himself never complained and Anglo-American relations were restored to their proper plane by the visit of Gerard Lambert's *Yankee* during the 1935 season, when *Endeavour* was top of the 'J' class.

During the 1935 season C. R. Fairey, owner of *Shamrock V* and Rear Commodore of the Royal London Y.C., tried to challenge with a 'K' or 'L' class yacht, but this was not accepted.

In 1936 *Endeavour II* appeared, a larger boat with greater displacement than her predecessor. She seemed to be faster, although she missed much of the season through losing two masts. The first *Endeavour* had been sold to H. A. Andreae, one of the *Sceptre* syndicate, but did not sail any too well.

Endeavour II was also designed by Charles Nicholson and built at Gosport. She was of the maximum waterline length of a 'J' boat, with a greater displacement than her predecessor. The sixteenth challenge was sent in the autumn of 1936, by the Royal Yacht Squadron. The challenger was not named, but it was agreed that her name would be given a month before the races were due to begin. A clear understanding was also reached on the vexed question of internal fittings.

The New York Y.C. were worried. Obviously a new defender was required, but no one seemed willing to form a syndicate. Vanderbilt therefore decided to order a new boat by himself. Her name was *Ranger*, built by the Bath Iron Works and designed as a result of exhaustive tank tests of models produced by Starling Burgess and Olin Stephens. The latter had produced some outstanding offshore racers and was in close touch with the tank tests being carried out at the Stevens Institute, at Hoboken, New Jersey. It was decided that each should design two sets of lines and the four models would be tested against those of *Rainbow*, *Weetamoe*, and *Endeavour I*, whose lines had been given by Charles Nicholson to Starling Burgess. The only stipulations were that each new boat was to be eighty-seven feet waterline and have a deep forefoot and preferably a moderate beam.

It appeared that in a 'J' boat the best performance was obtained by the greatest waterline, which increased her displacement, but for some reason seemed to retain light weather performance. This was proved by Vanderbilt who ballasted *Rainbow* down in the 1936 season to eighty-seven feet waterline to try her against *Yankee.*

The respective dimensions of the 'J' boat challengers and defenders mentioned in this chapter were as follows:

	Year First Commis-sioned	L.W.L. feet	L.O.A. feet	Beam feet	Draught feet	Displace-ment; tons	S. Area square feet
Enterprise	1930	80	120·9	22·1	14·6	128	7,583
Shamrock V	1930	81·1	119·1	19·8	14·8	134	7,540
Rainbow	1934	82	126·7	21	14·58	141·1	7,572
Endeavour I	1934	83·3	129·7	22·03	14·9	143·1	7,561
Endeavour II	1936	87	135·8	21·5	15	162·6	7,543
Ranger	1937	87	135·2	21	15	166	7,546

All rated 76 feet and all had centreboards.

It was found in the tank tests that a model of an eighty-seven feet waterline boat, with large displacement and wetted surface had been towed through the water more easily at all speeds than models of *Endeavour* and *Rainbow.* This model was *Ranger,* and the difference in her performance, contrary to expectations, was most pronounced at low speeds. Either this was a revolutionary model, or the old assumption of 'a little light boat for light weather', was erroneous. Although it has never actually been announced it seems to be general knowledge that *Ranger's* model was designed by Olin Stephens.

The new defender lost her mast on her first trip, while being towed from her builders to Newport, but a new one was soon ready. It is said to have cost £15,000. She was tuned up against *Yankee* and *Rainbow* and found to be very much faster.

Sopwith had asked for the races to be started on 31st July, hoping to find steady winds of fifteen to twenty knots.

As well as *Endeavour II,* the 1934 challenger was lent by

H. A. Andreae to F. Sigrist and P. Hill, as a trial horse, and even as the challenger if she sailed better than the new boat.

They sailed trials in the U.S.A. in which *Endeavour II* was definitely established as the better of the two. These trials were not necessarily races, the new boat often being put in bad positions and having to work herself out of them. This was severely criticized by some American yachting writers, who were trying to gauge the new boat's performance. They need not have worried.

The races, which started on 31st July, were so one-sided that they are not worth describing. A feature of the defender was her wardrobe of enormous quadrilateral jibs which had been evolved by Vanderbilt, and which were usually bigger and very much more effective than anything set by *Endeavour II*. It was to these sails first and the hull shape second that the owner of the defender attributed his success. He also remarked that as far as the crews were concerned, the challenger's was the more efficient, and that her helmsman and afterguard sailed her faultlessly. She was quite simply outclassed. *Ranger*'s time for the fourth race of the series, of 3 hours 7 minutes 49 seconds was a record, beating *Endeavour*'s set up in the second race of the previous series by 1 minute 12 seconds. Her decisive victory ensured the safety of the cup in the New York Y.C. once more, and it also killed the 'J' class, if indeed they had not already been dying through expense and oversparring.

The Royal Cutter *Britannia* had been scuttled off St. Catherine's Point on 10th July 1936, her owner King George V having died on 20th January of that year. The two *Endeavours* remained in American waters during 1937 taking part in the New York Y.C. cruise, but the 'J' class never raced again in British waters. It appeared that if ever the *America*'s Cup was to be raced for again it would have to be in a smaller boat. The total cost of building and running *Endeavour II* is said to have cost Mr. Sopwith a hundred and eight thousand pounds, a fortune in itself.

The Twelve Metres therefore took the place of the 'J' as the premier class in British waters. Several of the 'J' class owners bought these smaller boats so that in 1938 there was quite a strong class of six boats. V. M. MacAndrew's *Trivia* and C. R. Fairey's *Evaine* easily headed the list, with twenty and nineteen wins respectively, out of forty-seven races.

The Twelve Metres are built to the International Rule for vessels of that rating, and to the scantling requirements of Lloyd's Register of Shipping. The class first appeared on the Clyde in 1908, when two of the five boats in this country raced each other for the Olympic Gold Medal, the international element being the fact that one crew came from the Clyde and the other the Mersey! The present measurement formula can perhaps be understood from the simplified drawing which appears on page *xiii* of the Appendixes. The 'L' measurement is rather more complicated than that shown as it is subject to certain corrections concerned with girth, so that the 'L' figure for a Twelve Metre might be six to eight feet greater than the actual L.W.L.

The prospect of the visit of at least one American Twelve Metre to our shores in 1939 no doubt encouraged four owners to build new boats. They were Hugh Goodson's *Flica II*, designed by Laurent Giles (a new designer to the class) and built by Fife's at Fairlie, Sir William Burton's *Jenetta*, designed by Alfred Mylne and built at Ardmeleish, while Mr. Sopwith's *Tomahawk* and A. C. Connell's *Ornsay* were designed by C. E. Nicholson and built at Gosport. Interest in the class was intensified when it was known that the American visitor was H. S. Vanderbilt, with a new boat called *Vim*, designed by Sparkman and Stephens and built by H. E. Nevins. A sister planned by Gerard Lambert to be called *Vigour* never materialized.

The remaining boats were V. W. MacAndrew's *Trivia*, and Mr. C. R. Fairey's *Evaine*, and they were joined later in the season by *Blue Marlin* (W. R. Westhead).

The hull form of *Vim* and *Flica II* had been designed with the help of the test tank at the Stevens Institute, Laurent Giles testing possible models of the latter against that of *Evaine*.

Vim's keel was laid on 20th January 1939, and she was launched early in May for tuning up, in which she sailed three races without success, although she is said to have had bad luck in two of these, and given up to save her new canvas a wetting in the third. She was then shipped to England to start the season with the Twelves at Harwich on 10th June. In the opening race she led the fleet home by 2 minutes, but was disqualified for rounding a mark incorrectly. However, she won the next five, being defeated for the first time at Ramsgate on 20th June by *Evaine*.

Performance of the British Twelves seemed to improve as the season progressed, but even so when *Vim* sailed her last race at Southsea on 9th August, in which she was beaten by *Blue Marlin* (sailed by Colin Newman) by 13 seconds, she had won nineteen firsts, four seconds and two thirds out of twenty-seven starts. The season did not finish until 1st September and altogether forty-three races were sailed, twenty of them west of Portland Bill. The best British boat was *Tomahawk*, which won eleven firsts, eleven seconds and five thirds out of forty-one races.

Naturally the superiority of the American visitor gave rise to much comment in the yachting press. A correspondent in the *Yachting Monthly* writing under the pseudonym of 'Canvas' wrote quite early in the season:

'The visit of Vanderbilt's *Vim* is doing everybody concerned a power of good. My one regret is that *Vim* wasn't over here last year to interrupt the process of mummification which has been enveloping our 12 metre class.'

The correspondent concerned appeared, from his other writings, to be a staunch supporter of the R.O.R.C. so his view may have been a bit jaundiced, but it does suggest that the opposition might not have been particularly high class.

Various reasons were put forward for *Vim*'s superiority

Her hull did not appear to be very much faster than the British boats, but was certainly at no disadvantage at any time and was apparently superior to windward in a breeze. Major Brooke Heckstall-Smith considered that her body and centre of buoyancy lay somewhat further forward than that of our best boats, and those with discerning eyes, who have seen her lately, have remarked on her powerful shoulders.

She had an aluminium alloy mast, from which the upper cross trees and jumpers were discarded quite early in the season. It was considered that although the weight of this mast was much the same as the British wooden ones, the minimum weight being 1,000 lbs, it was about seventy per cent stronger than wood, and its deflection on lateral load was forty per cent less. In other words it stood up much better, and with less windage was infinitely superior. A high crown to the deck in the way of the mast gave a very slight increase in effective height of the sail plan, the limit being eighty-two feet from the deck. She was originally fitted with a Flettner rudder, but this was soon discarded. It seemed an impracticable fitting on grounds of cost and drag, while a properly balanced racing yacht should really never need such a device. How much her successes were owed to the mast we shall never know, but certainly she was able to set her genoa jibs more efficiently in a blow than her English rivals. Added to this was a general superiority in handling, particularly that of headsails and spinnakers, and one writer suggested that she lost little, indeed was even better than our boats, in pilotage.

The fact that she came three thousand miles and was obviously tuned up from the very first gives the lie to those who wring their hands and expect half a season in which to do it. Perhaps the factor that made the most difference was that H. S. Vanderbilt's afterguard consisted of Briggs Cunningham, Rod Stephens and 'Ducky' Endt. This combination, four good paid hands, and the very best that money could buy, certainly made our Twelve Metre owners think.

Unfortunately war broke out two days after the last race of the season, at Teignmouth on 1st September.

Vim went back to the States where there was racing for the class in September. As America did not enter the war until 1941 their Twelve Metre class had a further two seasons in which to gain experience, although no more were built.

PART TWO

THE SEVENTEENTH CHALLENGER BUILDING AND TRIALS

IV

The Challenge and Conditions for the Seventeenth Series

ON his return from the U.S.A., after the defeat of *Endeavour II* in 1937, Charles E. Nicholson expressed the opinion that it would be useless for any British boat to challenge for the cup, unless her model had been tank tested. The war which was brewing, and which followed, drove all but nostalgic thoughts of the Cup races from the minds of British yachtsmen. They may have happened to notice the hulls of the *Endeavours* lying at Camper and Nicholson's, Gosport.

In 1948, Captain J. H. Illingworth, the Commodore of the R.O.R.C., considered the possibility of renewing the struggle in an offshore racing type of boat. He was over in the States for the Newport–Bermuda Race with his famous *Myth of Malham*, and he and De Coursey Fales, then Commodore of the New York Y.C. agreed in principle that if the Cup races were ever restarted, they should be in an ocean racing type, which would be of value after the Cup races. This, however, came to nought as there was little chance of anyone on either side of the Atlantic being able to afford a vessel of at least sixty-five feet waterline, as required by the Deed of Gift. Even Sven Salen's beautiful *Bolero* is a mere fifty-one. At that time the Committee of the New York Y.C. were unable to recommend a change in the Deed, though this was strongly favoured by the two Commodores.

In 1953 a body called the Yacht Research Council was formed, mainly through the energetic efforts of that well-known North Norfolk sailor Jason Borthwick, who was chairman of the R.Y.A. Olympic Committee at the time. The aim of this body was to 'improve the breed' of British yachts by research into hull form, sails, and fittings. The necessity for something drastic to be done had been shown by the rather poor performance of the 1952 Olympic sailing team, Charles Currey excepted, at Helsinki. The Council only functioned for a couple of years, mainly financed by a gift of five thousand pounds from Harry Ferguson, the tractor manufacturer, and died rather surprisingly through lack of support from the yacht building industry, which it had been formed to assist.

A permanent result of the efforts of this body was the development of a tank testing technique based on that evolved by the late Professor Kenneth Davidson at the Stevens Institute, Hoboken, New Jersey. A 5·5 Metre, Owen Aisher's *Yeoman*, had been tested afloat and her successor was designed, and has since been modified, with the help of the tank at the National Physical Laboratory, Teddington. The Superintendent at the time, the late Dr. Charles Allan, had worked in his early career in Denny's of Dumbarton, where G L. Watson had tank-tested models for *Shamrock II*. He was also a great friend of Professor Davidson, who gave him much useful advice. Meanwhile tests had also been carried out on the hull form of a Dragon, at Saunders-Roe's tank at Osborne, Isle of Wight, supervised by Mr. W. A. Crago, to try the effects of changes in trim and displacement.

In April 1956 it was hinted in an American yachting journal called *The Skipper* that there was a possibility of a new *America*'s Cup Challenge. In July Commodore Henry Sears, of the New York Y.C., visited the Royal Yacht Squadron. He asked the Commodore, Sir Ralph Gore, whether the Squadron would be interested in a new challenge if the New York Y.C. obtained the approval of the U.S. Supreme Court to the necessary amendments to the Deed of Gift, to enable the Cup to be raced for in the International Twelve Metre class. The Twelve Metre was chosen as it was the largest pure racing class, although just a shade over half the waterline length of a 'J' boat.

The answer was that the Squadron was interested, but did not wish to be committed to a definite challenge at that stage. The Commodore announced that a new challenge might be made, under the amended deed, at the R.Y.S. August General Meeting in Cowes Week 1956.

Not all members were in favour of such a step. British yachting had undergone very great changes during the previous twenty years. The war and the economic state of the country had killed off all the larger classes. Even the Six Metres, which had sailed seventeen strong in the Olympic trials in Torbay, were reduced to a bare handful. Nearly all the sailing yachts of over fifty tons had been sold out of the country. Those whose winter Sunday afternoon pleasure was to admire the large yachts laid up in the Hamble, and at other centres, noticed the increasing emptiness of the mud berths.

With this thinning of large craft, paid hands became a dying race. There was not much future in a precarious life, in which ten pounds per week, with a retainer in the winter, was not easy to find, when that sum could perhaps be doubled in an aircraft factory or the docks. In the place of the large yachts had come an enormous number of small cruisers and the dinghies in their thousands. The latter tended to kill the source of good amateur crews, as ownership was within the reach of nearly everyone. There is little point in crewing for someone else when one can be one's own skipper.

Some of those who remembered the Cup races felt that they tended to breed ill feeling, and were slightly unfair. The record of British yachts against Americans in the previous few years had also been rather poor. In Cowes Week in 1955, when such craft as *Carina II* and *Harrier* had much of their own way, British owners were only just waking up to the fact that synthetic sailcloth was infinitely superior to cotton. Even then the issue tended to be clouded by some critics who attributed the American superiority to the fact that they were sailing centreboard boats. This was no new theory, in fact it has been argued inconclusively for over a century, but, as with the *America*'s cotton sails compared with the British flax, so some of the pundits doubted the superiority of Dupont's Dacron (or Terylene, I.C.I.'s equivalent) over cotton.

In that year our Six Metre team was beaten by the Americans, as they had been consistently since 1928, even though, by 1955, some or all had American Dacron sails. There was therefore quite a lot of defeatist thought as far as American yachts of any kind were concerned, which is only just being dispelled. In the 1956 Olympics our boats fared better than the American in all but the Star and Finn classes. By 1957, when most of our offshore racers were at last equipped with Terylene, they seemed to compare better with the Americans, indeed beat them in the R.O.R.C. Admiral's Cup, although *Carina II* repeated her 1955 Fastnet victory.

Hugh Goodson, a member of the Royal Yacht Squadron, and at that time Commodore of the Royal Dart. Y.C., had heard of the possibility of the alterations to the Deed of Gift, and decided to form a syndicate to build a challenger. He asked Lord Runciman, while they were sitting in Goodson's car outside the Royal Dart. Y.C. in September 1956, whether he would be interested. He was. They then both decided to ask a few friends to join them in what they called 'the project'.

The original members of the syndicate were: Hugh Goodson (Chairman), Viscount Runciman, H. A. Andreae, Bertram Currie, Group Captain Loel Guinness, Major H. W. Hall, Sir Peter Hoare, Major R. N. Macdonald-Buchanan, and Charles G. C. Wainman. They were joined at later stages by Viscount Camrose, Lieutenant-Colonel A. W. Acland, and Sir Joku Wardlaw-Milne, who had shown great interest from the beginning.

One of those approached by Hugh Goodson was not enthusiastic. This gentleman suggested, when told of the project, that he should see a psychiatrist!

All twelve members have contributed equally towards the building of the challenger and its maintenance. They have also brought to the periodic Syndicate meetings vast knowledge of various aspects of business and commerce, as well as of sport. Some have owned racehorses, and still do, so that they have been well equipped to face life's uncertainties.

All either own, or have owned, fine yachts. The Chairman was a very successful helmsman in the Twelve Metres with *Flica*, and before that, in the West Solent Restricted Class, of which he formed the Torbay Division in 1928. Lord Runciman sailed for the South in a blizzard the day after *Sceptre*'s launching in his twenty-four-tonner *Sandavore*, designed by Uffa Fox. It was Mr. Andreae, owner of *Candida* and then *Endeavour* of the 'J' Class, who gave up a season's sailing in the latter in 1937 to let her tune up her successor. Major Macdonald-Buchanan owns the old Twelve Metre *Kaylena*, as well as the 5·5 Metre *Sha Sha V*, which he has lent to promising helmsmen with Olympic aspirations from time to time. Group Captain Loel Guinness, one of the most enthusiastic exponents of the earliest possible challenge, has the 300-ton motor yacht *Calisto*.

Colonel Acland and Clarles Wainman are as well known at Bembridge, as Major Hall is as Commodore of the Royal Lymington Y.C. The latter owns the fast motor yacht *Ravahine*. Lord Camrose's father owned the 'J' boat *Cambria* and the fine steam yacht *Virginia*, while Bertram Currie has the fine cutter *Wind Star*, although he is perhaps better known for his prowess in the hunting field. I asked Sir Peter Hoare why they had all joined the Syndicate. 'We're all friends of Hugh,' he answered with a shy smile.

There was certainly no shortage of money, but to remedy a lack of up to date racing experience, they asked Lieutenant-Colonel R. S. G. Perry to act as technical adviser. A very experienced sailor, who had owned many boats, Perry represented this country in the 1952 and 1956 Olympics with his 5·5 Metres *Unique* and *Vision*. He won the Silver medal at

Melbourne with the latter, a boat which, her designer Arthur Robb is the first to point out, was full of her owner's bright ideas.

Perry called on Commodore Sears of the New York Y.C. on his way back from Melbourne in November 1956. Accompanied by Owen Aisher, who was at that time negotiating for the purchase of *Evaine*, they took a look at the famous *Vim*.

Evaine, a 1936 Nicholson-built Twelve Metre, was the only one of her class in this country not converted for cruising, although she had been laid up ever since 1939. Her previous owner, the late Sir Richard Fairey, is said to have kept her just in case something happened which would resurrect the class. Of the other Twelves in this country *Flica II* and *Vanity V* were converted for cruising and neither had ever been raced very successfully. *Kaylena*, built in 1929, was really a bit old for serious class racing, although she was a great asset for preliminary trials in 1957.

Of those which were available in 1939 *Tomahawk*, ironically enough, had been sold to an Italian owner a couple of years previously, by Sir Ralph Gore. *Little Astra* and *Blue Marlin* were also in the Mediterranean, *Trivia* (now *Norsaga*) in Norway, *Jenetta* in Canada, while *Westra* and *Ornsay* were victims of the blitz at Camper and Nicholson's, Gosport.

The Americans were not much better off. *Vim* remained, but she, *Gleam*, *Nyala* and *Nereus* had all been fitted out as cruisers. It was therefore obvious to Perry that if the challenge was to have the best chance, it would have to be made as soon as possible. The more the delay the more the Americans were liable to outbuild us. He therefore advocated the earliest possible challenge. There was a suggestion at this early stage that the syndicate should start by buying or chartering a Twelve Metre in the States, and have a season's racing over there in 1957 or 1958, the season before the challenge was actually to be decided. This was dismissed as impracticable as well as possibly bad for morale, as the crew and afterguard would probably have impressed on them ashore, if not on the water, the 'impossibility' of their task.

On 16th December 1956 the U.S. Supreme Court amended the Deed of Gift. The minimum waterline length was reduced to forty-four feet and the clause requiring the challenger to proceed to the race on her own bottom was deleted.

The syndicate wasted no time. Four designers, David Boyd, James McGruer, Charles A. Nicholson, and Arthur Robb were asked to submit two designs each for tank testing. Their terms of reference were wide, but actually limited by the International Twelve Metre rule. Meteorological data for the time of the races, issued by the U.S. Department of Commerce Weather Bureau, was made available to them. Their lines had to be ready by 1st April 1957. I went with them in a taxi from the Royal Thames Y.C. to the Royal Yachting Association Annual General Meeting, presided over by Prince Philip for the first time.

'Designed any good cup challengers lately?' I asked. They all grinned, said that they had been comparing notes, and one remarked on the appropriate completion date.

It was at this meeting that a well known dinghy sailor suggested, in a question to the President, that it was a pity that the vast amount of money, which would obviously be spent on the challenge, was not available for our Olympic effort; one club, he pointed out, was raising about £70,000, what were the others doing?

Even at this stage, although no challenge had yet been made officially, many of the pundits, particularly the disciples of offshore racing, were almost unanimous in their condemnation of the project and particularly the fact that the challenge was to be made in an International Twelve Metre. Writers in at least one British yachting journal even refused to believe that it would be in such a vessel. Some owners swore that had it been one of the new cruiser/racer type of Twelve Metre, whose waterline length just did not fit within the terms of the amended Deed of Gift, they would have built new boats. They were not interested in an 'old type Twelve Metre', because it was unsuitable for offshore racing after the Cup races, rating too high under the R.O.R.C. rule. The Syndicate ignored them. There had been much the same kind of criticism in the New York Yacht Club. It was considered that there were already plenty of events for offshore racers, in fact that branch of the sport had its own particular place in the international yachting scene. It was considered that there was still room for international match racing, in the largest possible racing class boat. Those in favour of this overrode some of the 'old guard', who suggested that the *America's* Cup should be left as a memorial to the 'J' boats and their even larger predecessors.

A New York Y.C. delegation visited London during April 1957, and the outline details of the challenge and conditions were thrashed out with the Royal Yacht Squadron. The challenge was made, dated 14th May, and the rest of the summer was spent in a somewhat lengthy correspondence finalizing these conditions, which are reproduced in full below.

CONDITIONS GOVERNING THE RACES FOR THE *AMERICA'S* CUP 1958

Conditions to govern the races for the *America's* Cup under the challenge of the Royal Yacht Squadron, dated 14 May 1957, for a Match in the International Twelve Metre Class, as agreed upon by the Committees of the Royal Yacht Squadron and the New York Yacht Club.

NOTE: Wherever time is referred to in these Conditions, it is Eastern Daylight Saving Time.

1 DATE OF RACES:

The first race shall be sailed on Saturday, September 20, 1958, and the races shall be sailed on every succeeding week-day; provided, however, that immediately on the conclusion of each race or upon a race being called off for the day, the Race Committee shall inquire of each contestant whether he is willing to start the next day. Should either contestant reply in the negative one day shall intervene before starting the next race. Sunday shall not count as such intervening day.

2 NUMBER OF RACES:

The Match shall be decided by the best four out of seven races.

3 COURSES:

Races shall start and finish at a mark anchored nine nautical miles S.S.E. (Magnetic) from the Brenton Reef Lightvessel and shall be sailed alternatively over windward and leeward and triangular courses of approximately twenty-four nautical miles in length.

The first race shall be to windward and leeward sailed twice around a course, the first leg of which shall be approximately six nautical miles to windward. The second race shall be triangular sailed over a course of approximately eight nautical miles to a leg, the first leg being to windward. The Magnetic courses shall be signalled and the tug bearing the marks shall be started not less than ten minutes prior to the warning signal.

4 START:

The warning signal, unless the race is postponed by the Race Committee, shall be made as nearly as practical at 11.00 A.M. and the starting signal at 11.10 A.M. No race shall be started after 1.10 P.M.

5 SIGNALS:

The warning signal shall be made ten minutes before the start.

Five minutes after the warning signal the preparatory signal shall be made.

Five minutes after the preparatory signal the starting signal shall be made.

The time of the starting signal shall be taken as the time of the start of both yachts.

6 POSTPONEMENTS:

The time of the warning signal shall not be postponed by the Race Committee except as follows:

a. In case of fog.

b. If, in its opinion, at the time appointed for the warning signal, the starting area is not sufficiently clear, or the wind is too light or too strong or the sea too rough reasonably to test the relative speed of the two yachts.
c. In case a yacht, after she has left her mooring for the start of a race and before the warning signal, is in a serious collision or accident, not the result of a defect in her hull or in her sails, rigging, gear, or the handling thereof; or in case the Race Committee is notified before the warning signal that a person on board has been seriously injured after the yacht left her mooring for the start.

The Instructions for the races shall specify the signals to be displayed in connection with postponements for the day or until later in the day, and where postponements are until later in the day, such postponements shall be for a period or periods of fifteen minutes. A copy of such Instructions shall be given to each yacht prior to the start of the Match.

7 TIME LIMIT:

If in any windward and leeward race neither yacht completes the course in six hours or in a triangular race in five and one-half hours, such race shall be resailed.

8 RACES RESULTING IN A TIE:

A race resulting in a tie shall be resailed.

9 NEW YORK YACHT CLUB RACING RULES TO GOVERN:

The Racing Rules of the New York Yacht Club as the same now exist shall govern the races, except in so far as the same may be inconsistent with the other provisions of this agreement, and particularly the provisions of Clause 10 hereof.

10 MEASUREMENT RULES OF THE INTERNATIONAL YACHT RACING UNION TO GOVERN:

The Measurement Rules of the International Yacht Racing Union including the Instructions to Measurers as published by the International Yacht Racing Union in 1939 and amended in 1950 (Instructions to Measurers No. 21) as submitted by the Royal Yacht Squadron to the New York Yacht Club by letter dated August 14, 1957 shall govern the races. The Table of Cabin Fittings and Schedule of Equipment in Rule

XVIa of the International Rule of Measurement and the Table of Sizes of Anchors, Chains and Warps in International Yacht Racing Union Rule No. 19 shall govern in so far as applicable to the Twelve Metre Class.

The Certificate of the Classification Society referred to in Rule XXII shall be the certificate of Lloyd's Register of Shipping and certificates hereafter granted shall be in accordance with its Rules and Regulations for the Construction and Classification of Yachts of the International Rating Classes as Reprinted by it with Revisions in 1949, which Revisions shall not apply to yachts now in existence and which have heretofore received such certificates.

Metal spars shall be permitted and structural items used but not required by the Rules may be of any material.

11 TIME ALLOWANCE:

There shall be no time allowance.

12 RATING:

Yachts shall not rate over Twelve Metres.

13 SELECTING THE CHALLENGING YACHT:

The challenger shall have the right to substitute another yacht for the yacht named in its challenge, provided that notice of its intention to do so shall be received by the challenged club at least one week before the date of the first race and that such other yacht shall in all respect comply with the terms of these Conditions.

14 SELECTING THE DEFENDING YACHT:

At least one week before the first race the Challenger shall be informed of the yacht selected to defend the Cup.

15 ACCIDENTS:

(1) In case a serious accident occurs to either yacht prior to the warning signal, she shall have such time, not exceeding in any event four weeks, as the Committees representing the two Clubs shall determine to be reasonable to effect repairs before being required to start, or if such accident occur after the warning signal, before being required to start in the next race; but no such allowance of time to repair shall extend the Match beyond October 31, 1958.

(2) If either yacht, except as provided in Clause 6, paragraph c, shall be disabled after leaving her mooring for the start of the race through a defect in her hull or in her sails, rigging, gear or the handling thereof, the other yacht shall start and continue the race.

(3) If through the fault of either yacht, the other be destroyed or so injured after the warning signal, as to be incapable of repair in time to complete the Match before November 1, 1958, and the yacht so destroyed or injured shall be free from fault, the Match shall be awarded to her.

16 DISQUALIFICATION:

If either yacht is disqualified in any race, such race shall be awarded to the other yacht, provided the race was completed within the time limit. The fouled yacht shall, however, be declared the winner if the Race Committee finds that her disablement caused by the foul prevented such completion.

17 REPRESENTATIVES:

Each Club shall by its Committee name a representative who shall have the right to be present at all measurements and shall have, when practicable, not less than twenty-four hours notice thereof. A representative of the challenger shall have the right to be on board the Race Committee boat during the races and may be consulted by the Race Committee in regard to the matters referred to in Clause 6.

18 MEASUREMENTS:

All measurements, except displacement, shall be taken or checked within two weeks of the commencement of the Match. Not less than seven days before the first race, the Measurement Certificates of both yachts signed by the Measurer of the New York Yacht Club shall be filed with the Secretary of that Club.

19 RE-MEASUREMENTS AND INSPECTIONS OF SIDE MARKS:

If either yacht in any way changes her L.W.L. or sail plan as officially taken she must obtain a re-measurement by special appointment before the next race, and must report the alteration to the Measurer and to the representatives of both Clubs at the New York Yacht Club Station at Newport by 9 P.M. of the day before the race following such alteration, and must arrange with the Measurer for re-measurement and, if required, be in Brenton Cove by six (6) o'clock A.M. of the day of said race, and be at the disposition of the Measurer until seven (7) o'clock A.M. if necessary for purposes of re-measurement.

If either yacht shall take in or remove ballast or dead weight, she must notify the Measurer and the representatives of the two Clubs and be at the disposition of the Measurer, for inspection of marks. The representatives of the two Clubs shall have the right to be present at all re-measurements and inspections of marks and shall be given such notice thereof as time may permit, such notice to be delivered at the Club Station at Newport.

All measurements certified to by the Measurer shall be final and not be subject to protest by either party. In the event of the Measurer being unable to obtain a measurement which he considers accurate before a race, a re-measurement shall be taken as soon as possible after the race.

20 DECISIONS OF RACE COMMITTEE:

The decisions of the Race Committee of the New York Yacht Club in all matters pertaining to the Racing Rules shall be final and there shall be no appeal therefrom.

ROYAL YACHT SQUADRON.
October 10, 1957. NEW YORK YACHT CLUB.

One of the points raised, which caused quite a lot of trouble at the time, was a suggestion that it might be possible for the Americans to build a centreboard Twelve Metre, but this is not permitted by the class rules. Some wanted to restrict the foot measurement of the spinnakers. In the International Twelve Metre rule there is a restriction on the measurement of the luffs of the spinnaker, but the foot is unlimited. The result has been some very large spinnakers, which are very difficult to control. Sir Ralph Gore pointed out that this would not only be undesirable, but also impracticable within the time.

V

Tank Tests

THE four designers worked in a state of friendly rivalry. No doubt in the back of the minds of all but Arthur Robb, who had no connexion with any yard, there must have been the possibility of landing the best yacht-building job of 1957. All four had designed successful boats.

David Boyd had the Seawanhaka Cup winners *Circe* and *Titia* to his name, as well as a number of other good Six Metres and a couple of 5·5s. His first creation was the beautiful 34-ton yawl *Zigeuner*.

James McGruer, one of the well-known Clyde boat-building family, was responsible for *Johan*, the 1948 British Olympic Six Metre, and others of her class. He was among the first to try his hand with the Eight Metre Cruiser/Racer Class. For a time he worked in the U.S.A. for L. Francis Herreshoff, the son of the 'Wizard of Bristol'. He and Charles A. Nicholson are technical advisers to the International Yacht Racing Union.

'Young' Charlie, nephew of the great Charles E. Nicholson, designer of the last four challengers, had made quite a name for himself with offshore racers such as *Lothian* and *Yeoman*. The latter and also a couple of 5·5 Metres of the same name were designed for Owen Aisher. It was one of the great yachting tragedies that most of the records of the famous yacht-building firm of Camper and Nicholson were actually lost in the blitz, but even so, this firm, of which Charles runs the Southampton branch, probably has a greater accumulated knowledge of racing yacht design than most on this side of the Atlantic.

Arthur Robb, a New Zealander, who spent some time before the war working for Morris and Lorimer's of Sandbank, designed *Vision*, the 5·5 Metre Silver Medal winner at Melbourne. He considers that his *Uomie*, a successful offshore racer which competed in the 1958 Bermuda Race, was one of his best efforts. He also designed *Kahurangi*, built in New Zealand in 1952, to the Twelve Metre Cruiser/Racer rule.

The models were built at Souter's Yard, Cowes, to the scale of 1 inch to 1 foot. They were of pine in layers, or 'bread and butter fashion' as it is known amongst model yachtsmen. They cost £150 each. With them was also one of *Flica II*. She was a Twelve Metre which had been built in 1939, by Fife's of Fairlie, to designs by Laurent Giles for Hugh Goodson. She never fared particularly well in her first season, suffering rather more than her fair share of teething troubles. She had a large foretriangle, which proved a 'killer' for her crew in Solent conditions, and which was considered to have been a mistake. Her model had been tested at the Stevens tank at Hoboken, N.J., and had been found to be slightly better than that of *Evaine*. The Stevens tank data on her was still available and as she was the only British Twelve Metre to have been tank tested, it was obvious that the new models should be tried against her. Some criticized this move, but can take comfort in the fact that the new models were all superior. Incidentally it was a photograph of *Flica*'s tank model which appeared, labelled *Sceptre*, in an American magazine and an English daily newspaper in company with those of the four potential American defenders in March 1958.

There had been a quite unofficial suggestion that the four designers should try one orthodox and one unorthodox model, but to the layman's eye all appeared to be pretty normal metre boats, except for one of Charles Nicholson's. She had a 'cod head' type of bow and would have had a bowsprit had she ever been built. She was quite a favourite with some of those who saw the models while they were being made.

As already mentioned, an earlier challenger had been

designed with the help of the test tank. This was in 1901, when G. L. Watson, assisted by Mr. Denny of Dumbarton, experimented for nine months, testing eleven models, before he settled on the one which became *Shamrock II.* The tank was at Denny's and was designed by Professor William Froude, who designed the Admiralty experimental tank at Haslar. The models in those days were made in the same way as those used for big ship model tests, of paraffin wax over a core of lath and canvas. After *Shamrock II's* first race, an American is reported to have remarked that the important factor which Mr. Watson's tests lacked was a model of *Columbia*, against which to try his creations. Nowadays the cynics merely remark that one cannot tank test the helmsman!

Nat Herreshoff always designed his boats by making models of them, developing them by eye rather than from line drawings. Charles E. Nicholson took a great interest in model yachting, being a frequent spectator at Gosport model yacht pond, where many of his employers raced boats which they had built.

It was not until 1937, however, that the test tank as we know it today made itself felt in the cup races. The defender, *Ranger*, was perhaps the ultimate 'J' boat. She was tried against the model of *Endeavour*.

The technique used by the Saunders-Roe test tanks of which William A. Crago is the Superintendent, is kept as flexible as possible so that results from other research or theoretical work can rapidly be taken into account. For the tests on the *Sceptre* models, the procedure was agreed between the Syndicate, Mr. Crago, and the four designers, at a meeting on 31st January 1957. The assumption had to be made that the centre of effort of the sail plan of all the models was at the same height above the waterline. It was also decided that the 'Gimcrack' sail coefficients should be used, as they had been found to be sufficiently reliable by the Yacht Research Council's full scale tests on the 5·5 Metre *Yeoman*

IV. The tank tests were carried out in calm water, because any attempt to introduce accurate rough water conditions would have made the technique very complicated and interpretation of the results doubtful.

Each model floated at its designed waterline and was ballasted so that the position of the centre of gravity corresponded with that of the full-sized vessel. Small studs to produce turbulence were fitted to the forepart of the underwater body and can be seen in the photograph between pages 36 and 37.

In tank testing the models are towed down the tank by a special dynamometer mounted on a carriage. The dynamometer is attached by means of an air bearing to the top of a stump mast, which is the point assumed to be the centre of

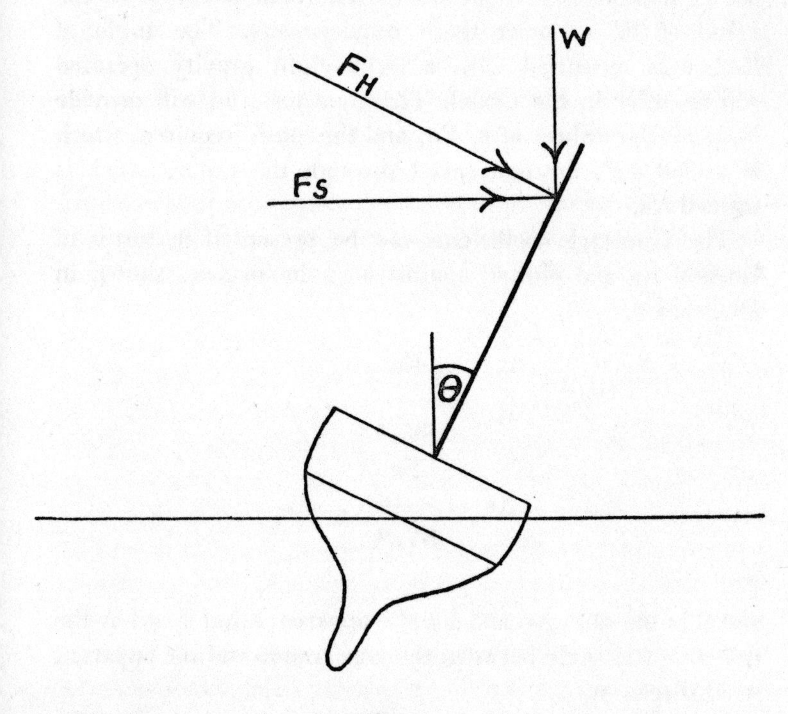

Diagram 2

the aerodynamic forces (or centre of effort) of the yacht's sail plan. The model is free to heel and is forced to make leeway, by an applied couple whose downward force is vertical. A further vertical downward force is applied at the centre of action of the aerodynamic forces (i.e. the top of the stump mast). Apologies are made for the technicalities of this and the next page or two, but tank testing is a highly complicated business. With reference to Diagram 2, on page 65, the dynamometer measures the force F_S, whilst the vertical force W is applied by means of weights, and the first test requirement is that the resultant of F_S and W should be normal to the mast. The value of this resultant is F_H. As perhaps can be imagined such conditions do not occur necessarily during the first test run down the tank, but the use of special equipment allows the rapid isolation of the value of W to meet these requirements. The angle of heel θ is measured with a lightweight gravity operated roll recorder in the model. Thus one test run will provide in particular values of θ, F_H, and the 'push' required, which is called F_R^1, for one speed through the water, which is termed V_S.

The Gimcrack coefficients can be presented in terms of K_H and K_R and plotted against θ in the manner shown in Diagram 3,

$$\text{Where } K_H = \frac{F_H}{SV_A^2} \quad \ldots . \ 1$$

$$K_R = \frac{F_R}{SV_A^2} \quad \ldots . \ 2$$

and S is the sail area and V_A the apparent wind speed at the sail. B is the angle between the true course and the apparent wind direction.

Now, from the measured value of θ unique values of K_H

and K_R can be deduced from Diagram 3. From this value of K_H and the measured value of F_H equation 1 can be used to calculate V_A (or apparent wind speed). The value V_A can then be employed with equation 2 together with the values of K_R to deduce F_R.

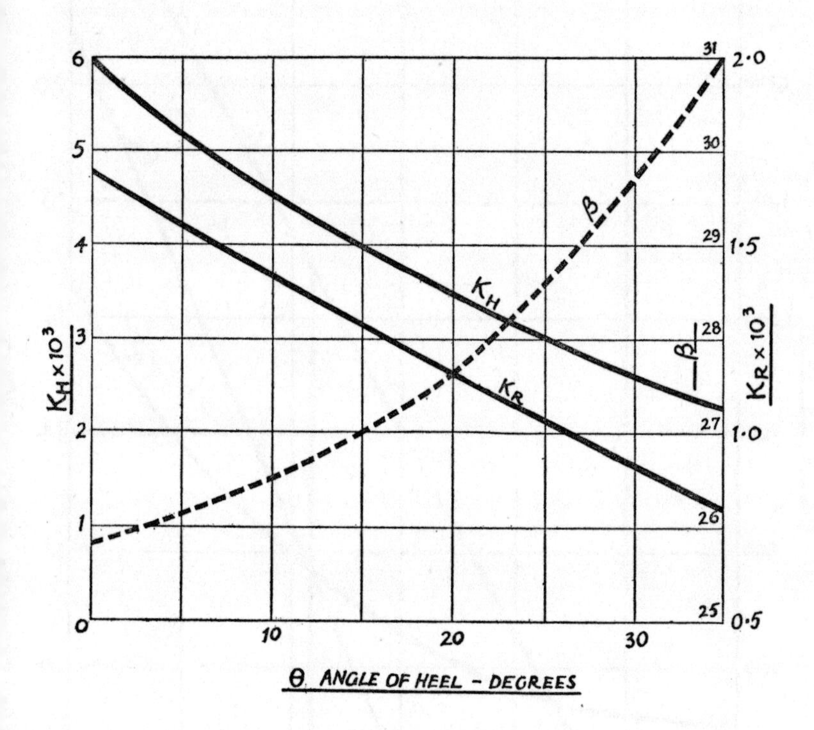

Diagram 3

It is important to realize that F_R is the 'push' force that can be developed by the sail, whilst F_R^I is the value actually measured during the test. In general it will be found that F_R^I (after correction for scale effect) will not in fact be equal to F_R and hence the condition actually tested will not be a true sailing condition. Therefore several heel angles are tried and a cross plot produced as shown in Diagram 4.

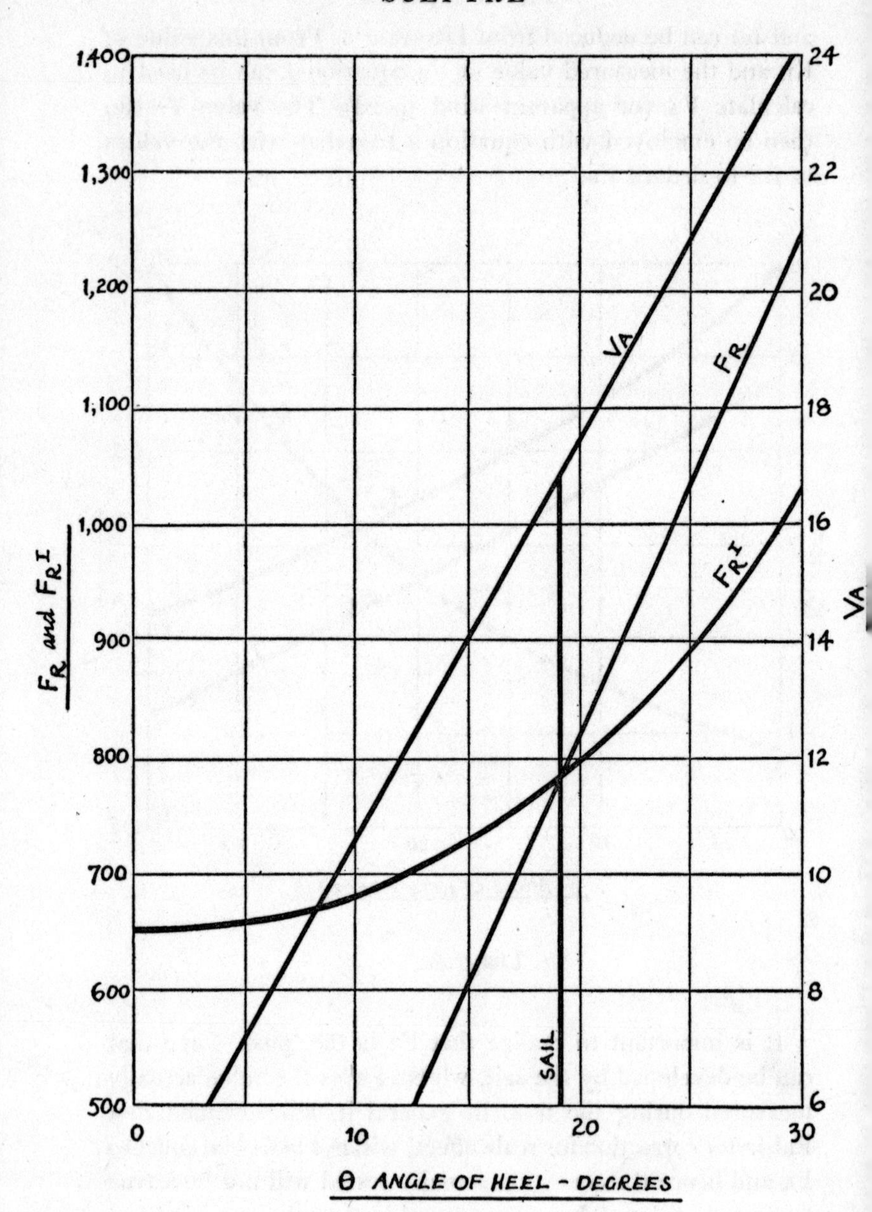
1,400
1,300
1,200
1,100
1,000
900
800
700
600
500
24
22
20
18
16
14
12
10
8
6
0
10
20
30
F_R and F_R^I
V_A
V_A
F_R
F_R^I
SAIL
Θ ANGLE OF HEEL - DEGREES

Diagram 4

The intersection of the F_R line and F_R^I line corresponds to a θ and V_A value, where the craft is actually sail propelled, and this is the position which it is necessary to isolate. Furthermore the final value of θ determined from the cross plot corresponds to a 'sailing' value of β from Diagram 3. It is now possible to calculate the true wind speed and the speed made good to windward as follows—the Vector diagram for a sailing craft is as shown in Diagram 5, where, in addition to the symbols already defined we have:

V_T the true wind speed and
V_{MG} the speed made good to windward.

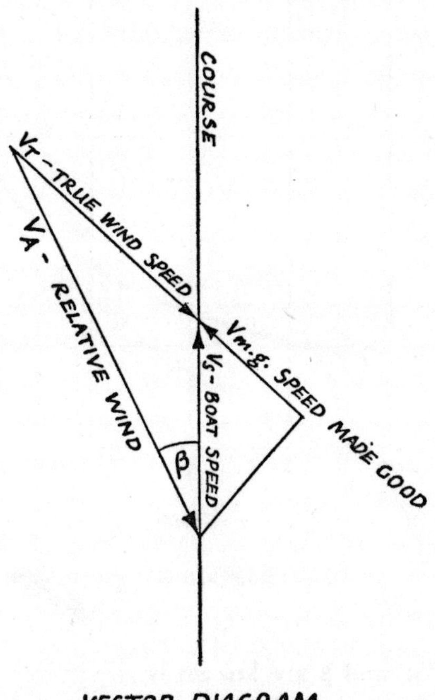

Diagram 5

From the diagram it is possible to show that

$$V_T^2 = V_A^2 = V_S^2 - 2V_A V_S \cos \beta \ldots 3.$$

$$\text{and } V_{MG} = V_S \cos \left[\sin^{-1} \left\{ \frac{V_A \sin \beta}{V_T} \right\} \right]$$

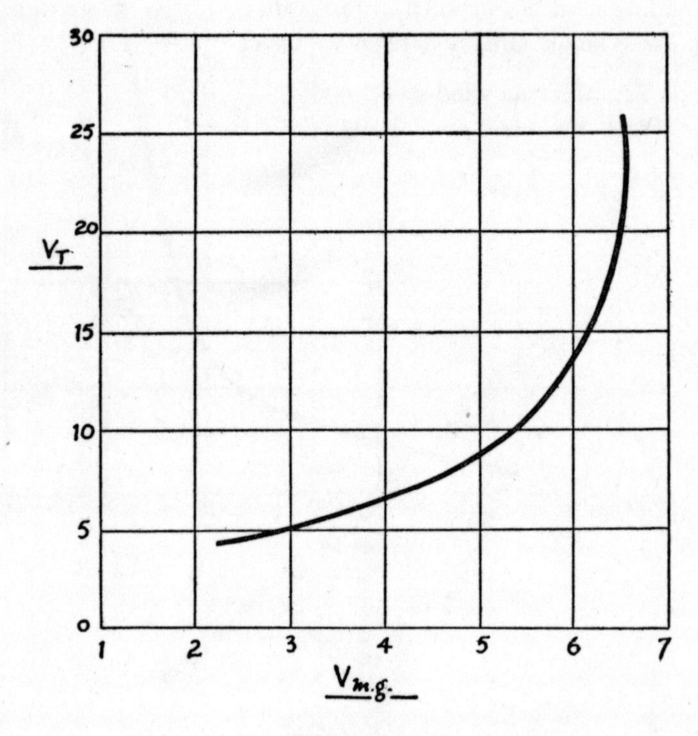

Diagram 6

Since V_A, V_S, and β are known it is possible to calculate V_T and V_{MG}. These can then be presented as shown in Diagram 6. Such graphs were produced for each boat after about sixty runs in the tank. The upright resistance can also be measured, a further fifteen runs being necessary. This upright resistance curve, Diagram 7, with Diagram 6 form the 'hull characteristics' from which assessments can be made of the hull's efficiency.

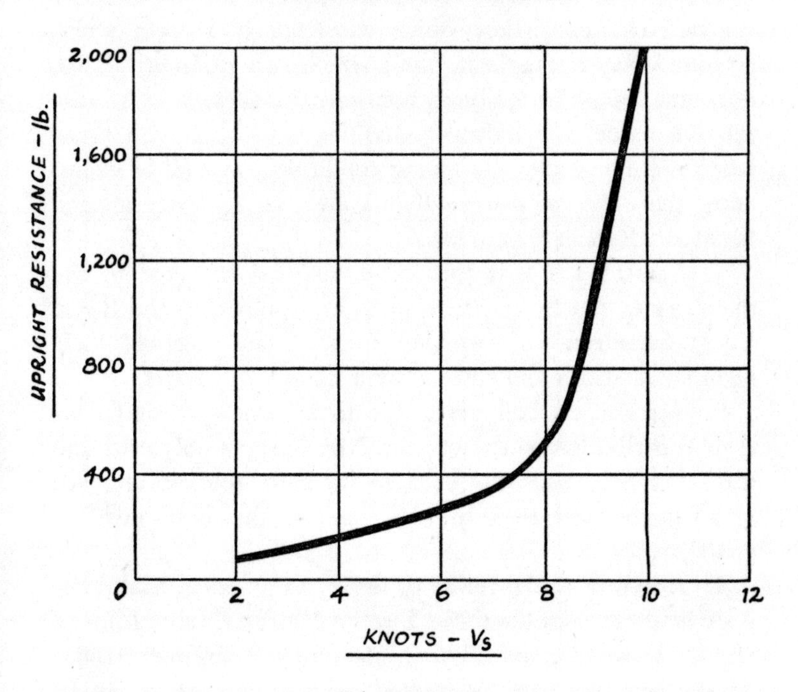

Diagram 7

The test runs started on 6th June 1957 and were carried out every night by Norman Bromfield and various assistants under the supervision of Mr. Crago. I had a ride on the carriage during a test run on the model of *Flica II* one evening, and was impressed most of all by the astonishing way in which leeway was noticeable, perhaps because it was exaggerated by the angle of heel.

The tank results were analysed by a committee consisting of Mr. Crago, Hugh Goodson, Lieutenant-Colonel Perry and Frank J. Murdoch. The choice of the latter was made by mutual agreement between the four designers. He had been technical adviser to Sir Thomas Sopwith in the two *Endeavours* and he had also raced with him in *Tomahawk* in 1939. He was himself a very successful Six Metre helmsman, notably in *Lalage* and *Marletta*. His main function was to translate the hull characteristics, which were not in a form which provided easy comparison, into a simple order of merit. This, of course, involved applying non-scientific factors such as the relative value of windward qualities compared with those when running under cup racing conditions, as well as evaluating the effect of the weather known to be likely around Brenton's Reef in September.

The result was that this sub-committee reported to the members of the Syndicate who had assembled at the Royal Yacht Squadron on 13th July 1957. They accepted their recommendations and chose David Boyd's 'B' model.

Saunders-Roe's had given the tank tests without fee as their contribution to the project. Mr. Crago's only criticism was that the tank was used solely as a 'referee' and not as an instrument to help evolution of the best possible model.

To return from the realm of theory to practice, trial races were held between the three Twelve Metres *Evaine*, *Flica II* (H. R. Attwood), and *Kaylena*, starting in midsummer 1957. As the last two were converted for cruising and dragging propellors, they usually formed a stately procession soon after the start. However, they gladdened the hearts of the old-timers, who regretted the passing of the larger classes. They also gave a number of crews and helmsmen, selected by the syndicate, a chance to become accustomed to handling vessels of that size. They were sometimes joined by the older ex-Twelves, *Vanity* (Capt. M. P. R. Boyle) and *Iyruna* (J. A. G. Boyden), although the sail plans of these two were cut down so much that they were usually left miles astern.

During Cowes Week Colonel Perry resigned his position as technical adviser. He had his own very definite ideas on the whole project and, feeling that his advice was not being taken, considered that the syndicate should find someone else before the building of the challenger started.

Before the designer had been chosen Perry had suggested to Goodson that it was important to get a Twelve Metre to sail at the end of the season quite alone. This would be for the provisional crew and chosen designer to work out the best deck layout, decide on spinnaker gear, and various other technical matters concerned with sailing the *America's* Cup races in general and the equilateral triangle in particular.

An open water course was essential to teach the helmsman and navigator the technique which they would have to adopt. The chosen designer was to be on board, and the builder, if indeed he was not the designer. Sails particularly required were a large Terylene genoa and a very large spinnaker, to test gear. It was hoped to try to set a second headsail inside the genoa in certain conditions, and also to work out a drill and find suitable gear for changing from large to small spinnakers. Such navigational problems as the angle through which a Twelve Metre tacks could be solved, and the difficult problem of tacking downwind explored.

The scope of these trials was enlarged to include crew trials with three boats in Torbay. In spite of having resigned, Perry remained to organize this party, adhering as well as he could to his original plans. It was decided that *Flica II* should act as *Sceptre* and that *Evaine* would play her part as a trial horse, with *Kaylena* spare. The boats were delayed by bad weather on their voyages from the Solent, while two of the marks which had been laid by R. N. College, Dartmouth, had been removed by French fishing boats.

Racing eventually started on Monday, 19th August, and some quite useful work was done, including starting practice, which has been a feature of *Sceptre's* working up. Various helmsmen were tried including Hugh Goodson, Lieutenant-Colonel W. T. Towers-Clark, Owen Aisher, Commander Sam Brooks, Lieutenant-Commander Graham Mann, while quite a lot of other talent was in attendance, including Uffa Fox. At that time the only firm members of *Sceptre*'s crew were R. Llewellyn (navigator), J. Slorance (professional skipper), and P. Thornycroft.

David Boyd arrived on the Wednesday, sailing in *Evaine* that day and *Flica II* the next. He had not sailed in a big racing boat for some time and those two days helped to remind him of the immense power required to sail a Twelve Metre.

Evaine left on the Friday, leaving *Flica II* and *Kaylena* to race in Brixham Tower regatta.

It was at the start of this race that Hugh Goodson was knocked on the head and swept overboard, when the strop on the boom holding the mainsheet block failed. Sam Brooks, who was sailing with him, dived overboard to hold him up, until both were picked up. *Flica* had sailed round unaware of the accident.

Brooks was awarded the Royal Humane Society's testimonial on vellum for his gallant effort. His exertions in the water made him decide to give up smoking!

As the weather was bad and a lot of people were fed up Perry ordered a stop to the trials. There is no doubt that they were of immense value to David Boyd and to some of those who sailed in the two boats, but much of the necessary gear was not available. There were three boats instead of the original one, making the whole thing too complicated. It had also been hoped that the apparent winds on the reaching legs of the equilateral triangular course could have been found, but this was never done. The difficulties of helmsman-navigator communication were not studied. Last but not least, it was thought by some that Brixham was too far away from sailmakers, yachtsman's homes, and yards accustomed to Twelve Metre type gear, for trials of that sort. These require a dictator and a strong sailing committee with a properly organized course.

A friend, who was in one of the boats during these trials, told me that he found that an almost infallible way of judging whether the helmsman was any good was to lie up by the forestay, watching the luff of the jib and feeling the movement of the bow. He recommended this, in the same way that some maintain that the only place from which to watch rugger is from behind the goalposts.

The injury to Hugh Goodson was a considerable set-back to the project as he was undoubtedly the leader of the syndicate. He was confined to bed for several weeks and the general day-to-day running of the syndicate fell on the capable shoulders of Charles Wainman.

Sails were quite a problem. British weavers had lagged behind the Americans in the manufacture of synthetic sail-cloth, such as Terylene, particularly in the heavier weights suitable for a Twelve Metre. Enough American Dacron was therefore bought from the U.S.A. to make a trial mainsail for *Evaine*. It was this mainsail which was set by *Sceptre* on her first trials and which was severely criticized by many who saw it. By the look of the leech it had received a pretty severe testing.

A very large spinnaker was ordered from Jean-Jacques Herbulot, during the 5·5 Metre class races for the Coppa d'Italia in Poole Bay. This remarkable Parisian, an architect by profession and a well-known small boat sailor, had found a very excellent shape for a spinnaker, and with his wife and daughter had made such sails for many of the 5·5 and Six Metres. *Evaine*'s was the largest they had made and they had to borrow a ballroom in which to lay it out.

It was set by *Evaine* off the Needles in September, in conditions of great secrecy, but Sam Brooks, who was in America at the time to reconnoitre the course off Newport, was told all about it in the New York Y.C. a few days later.

Sam Brooks, Ross Llewellyn, and T. A. H. Beddington had been sent across to the U.S.A. in September 1957 to have a look at the conditions at Newport, Rhode Island, both ashore and afloat. They sailed in a chartered boat, *Sora III*, over the Cup course, noticing particularly the big ocean swell.

They watched the two American Twelve Metres, *Vim* and *Gleam*, racing against each other, and were impressed by the smartness with which the crews of both boats sheeted home their large genoas when tacking.

They were there for about a fortnight, and there is no doubt that the visit was of great value, both from the sailing point of view and also from that of Tommy Beddington, who had taken charge of all shore arrangements. Most of all it impressed the Americans, who remarked on the obvious seriousness of the new challenge.

VI

The Building of Sceptre

AS David Boyd was the managing director of the firm of Alexander Robertson and Sons of Sandbank, Argyll, his yard was the fairly obvious choice to build the challenger. Boyd had joined it as designer twenty-three years before, at the age of thirty-two, from Fife's of Fairlie. Every yacht he has designed shows that this tall silvery-haired Scot, with the deep voice and clear blue eyes, is following in the great tradition of those artists of yacht architecture. David Boyd probably could not design an ugly yacht if he tried.

The yard was founded by the late Alexander Robertson, in 1876, when he started hauling boats up the beach, at Sandbank, on the south side of the head of the Holy Loch. The present chairman is George Robertson, the founder's son, while George's nephew Alastair is also a director. Robertson's have always enjoyed a great reputation for craftsmanship, as I can personally testify, having once owned the Dragon *Primula*, built by them in 1937. They built some of the earliest Twelve Metres, as well as many smaller racing craft. For many years they have built lifeboats for the R.N.L.I. and during the war some of the finest coastal force craft for the Royal Navy came from Sandbank. During 1957 they built a handsome 42-ton ketch for Colonel Whitbread, called *Lone Fox*, to designs by Robert Clark. They therefore had recent experience of a yacht of about the size of a Twelve Metre.

The seventeenth challenger was undoubtedly something very special. She was to be the boat to win the *America*'s Cup, which was the sole object of the Syndicate. She was therefore to be regarded as expendable. As no other vessel of her class had been built since 1939, there was little to guide her designer. The only man alive who had designed a Twelve Metre was Olin Stephens, of America. Standing with a roll of plans under his arm, on the deck of the ferry from Dunoon to Gourock, David Boyd explained: 'You can't just open a catalogue and order fittings for a Twelve Metre. We have had to start from scratch.'

It was the same with the boat herself. There was only the brief experience of a few weeks' racing in 1957 and the results of Sam Brooks's observations in the U.S.A. to guide the Syndicate and designer. There was the great help and advice of Hugh Goodson, Colonel Perry and Owen Aisher, while the members of the syndicate had bright ideas, as did their friends. Boyd's friends gave advice, as did other well-wishers. All this had to be sorted out, the good separated from the bad, the practicable from the impracticable. Some might have been good, but would have taken too long. Time was vital. With one single boat, against the three or four which were rumoured to be building in America, she had to be ready in April to give the crew a chance.

Before the building of a yacht can be started there are numerous necessary preliminaries. The designer's drawings have to be laid out, full size, on the mould loft floor. Materials have to be ordered, in this case timber from four different firms, the steel frames, and lead for the keel to name a few. The pattern for the keel must be made and the hundred and one other things which fit together to make a racing yacht must be thought of. In view of the nature of the job, a veil of secrecy was thrown round the yard. Visitors were regarded with suspicion and the building shed was open only to those working on the challenger. This also gave Head Foreman Sam Auld and his team of craftsmen (whose names are in Appendix C) a chance to work without strangers breathing down their necks. Auld, seventy-three years of age when *Sceptre* was completed, had worked at Robertson's for forty-five years.

By early October there were signs of activity in the building shed. The mahogany keel assembly was being shaped, parts of it with that most fascinating of all shipwrights' tools, the adze.

On 10th October 1957 all was ready for the casting of the lead keel. It was a still, dull day as we passed the yard to try to fish a very stagnant Loch Eck. Smoke was pouring out of the furnace chimney vertically into the autumn gloom. Casting a keel is hot work. The molten lead was run into the mould, a few golden sovereigns and half crowns went in too, for luck, and the next morning only a few 'dead marines' and a large mass of lead remained to show that work on the challenger had really begun.

The mild steel frames arrived from Millen Brothers of Paisley and gradually the boat began to take shape. By December the backbone was complete; the keel assembly, the alternate steel and laminated oak frames, the spruce shelf and the bilge stringer were all in place and the African mahogany planking was laid over the fair curves of the challenger's hull. This was completed on the 12th February 1958, when the Press were allowed into the shed for the first time, to admire David Boyd's creation and the superb craftsmanship.

'She's beginning to look like a boat,' he said. He had worked and continued to work fourteen hours a day, chasing suppliers and ironing out the day-to-day snags which were inevitable. He is a keen wildfowler, but told me that he hardly had time to lift a gun the whole season during which *Sceptre* was being built. His men, too, were often working overtime, but one could not help noticing the immense pride which they were taking in their work.

After a brief glimpse through it, the veil of secrecy was discreetly replaced for the fitting out and completion. A frequent privileged visitor to the shed, however, was J. Herbert Thom, who won and defended the Seawanhaka Cup in 1938 and 1939 with his Six Metre *Circe*, built by Robertson's. She was David Boyd's first metre boat design and there was no doubt that every man who built *Sceptre* would have liked to have seen Thom given the helm.

Much thought had been given to the equipment for the boat. Hugh Goodson had fully recovered from his accident and by November was back in the chair of the Syndicate. A technical adviser was badly needed and Sam Brooks, who had been over to the U.S.A. with the reconnaissance party, filled the breach. An ex-submariner, who had become a Naval Work Study specialist, he was admirably suited to give the practical seaman's point of view. He had owned a National 12-foot dinghy while at R.N. College, Dartmouth, and since the war had had much offshore racing experience in the 100-square-metre *Marabu*. He had skippered her in the 1952 Bermuda and Transatlantic races. A technically minded fellow, his hobby was making fishing-rods, and very good ones too.

Ross Llewellyn, who had originally been earmarked for the job as navigator, decided that he could not spare the whole of the 1958 summer away from his farm, so asked to be released. In his place Sam's brother, Joe Brooks, was invited. He was also in the Navy, a Lieutenant-Commander. He had been a midget submariner and in 1956 had lost both feet as a result of an underwater explosion. He was reluctant to accept because of his comparative immobility, although he had sailed in the 1957 Channel and Fastnet races. Eventually he did so and got down to the problem of suitable navigational equipment for the races and the tuning up. He fought a light-hearted running battle with David Boyd, who repeated almost every time he saw him:

'I'll have none of your rubbish aboard.'

It had been decided by the syndicate to call their challenger *Sceptre*. The name aroused speculation as to its origin. The instrument is one of the symbols of sovereignty, and the name was once borne by a famous racehorse. It was thought of by Charles Wainman, who is reported to have said that they wanted a name that would not look too silly if the boat did not win. There was a wartime submarine of that name which, by a strange coincidence, was that which towed a midget submarine in which Joe Brooks was serving to a successful raid on Bergen.

Once the hull structure was complete and to the satisfaction of Lloyd's Register of Shipping, with whose rules for classification and building all Twelve Metres must comply, the completion of the boat progressed. The main problem had always been to save weight. This is particularly vital in such things as the deck and the fittings on it. The greater the ratio of the weight of the keel to that of the total displacement the better in a racing boat. For this reason the external and internal fittings and the furnishings had to be as light as possible. Here again Lloyd's Register had to give advice on such problems as the permitted materials for bulkheads.

As examples of the lengths to which this weight saving was carried, the deck collar for the mast and the steering gear quadrant were both aluminium alloy. The 25·3-gallon fresh water tank, required by the class rules, was aluminium, as were the handrail clips along the foredeck. The rail itself was a Tufnol tube with the spinnaker boom downhaul led through it. The table legs and the pipe cot frames were also aluminium, the wash-basin plastic and the Blake W.C. was an aviation model, as originally designed for the Short flying-boats. The castings for this were aluminium alloy and the pipes polythene. The outlet through the hull was sealed by a spring loaded valve, so that when the W.C. was not being flushed, the hull surface was unbroken by the aperture.

The cabin and cockpit flooring was of the same aluminium alloy, bonded to a balsa wood backing, which is used in airliners. Tufnol was used for the rudder tube, bearings, and also for the most impressive steering wheel, the operation of which has to be 'finger light'.

The pine decking looked as if it was laid in the conventional manner, with the planks following the covering board. A sheet of plywood was, however, laid over the spruce deck beams and the planking laid on top of that. The seams between the planks were caulked with the special British Paints P.R.C. compound, resulting in complete watertightness.

The mast was designed by David Boyd. It was thought at one stage that it would probably be made by the Hawker Siddeley Group, but this proved impracticable. They did, however, subject the design to examination by their stress experts, before it was passed on to Camper and Nicholson's late in January 1958. This famous yacht-building firm had more experience than any other in the country of the building of large metal masts. By almost superhuman efforts and fine teamwork they produced the finished mast in time for the launching.

It was a 91-foot spar, pear-shaped and built up in sections, alternately riveted together on one side and screwed on the other. A normal alloy female track was fitted to the after side. Nicholson's had the material, to Northern Aluminium's specification N.S. 6, in stock. It was to be supported by main shrouds, cap shrouds led over one set of cross trees only, and a pair of jumper stays. In other words the rigging plan was to be the same as that of a Dragon. The thickness of the walls was $\frac{1}{4}$ inch as far as the cross trees, $\frac{3}{16}$ inch from there approximately to the jumper struts and $\frac{1}{8}$ inch at the top. The minimum weight of a Twelve Metre mast is 1,000 lbs, and I am told that this one was very close to it. The centre of gravity must be at least 31·1 feet from the deck.

The solid shrouds were made from special high tensile bars, with the centre portion cold rolled to a true streamlined section. The lower shrouds were approximately 36 feet long, with the cap shrouds in two parts, the lower about 35 feet and the upper 24 feet 6 inches. They were fitted with the necessary fork ends to suit the mast fittings. It was considered that although stranded wire rigging would have the necessary strength, at a saving in weight, it was too elastic, permitting too much movement of the mast under wind stresses.

In the early stages the light weight of titanium was considered and Brunton's of Musselburgh, who were making a gift of the rigging to the Syndicate, already had experience in the fabrication of this special metal. They were also in a position to produce it in streamlined sections, but it was also found to be too elastic for the purpose. It was therefore decided that high tensile steel was the most satisfactory and could be accepted in view of the expendable nature of the challenger. The cadmium coating, which the shrouds were given, did not last very long on the lower sections, giving them a rather unsightly appearance until renewed.

Brunton's had pioneered the manufacture and application of streamlined sections for the external bracing of aircraft, and as long ago as 1907 had supplied them to the British Government. Notable examples of their application were the airships R.100 and R.101 and Schneider Trophy aircraft. Brunton's also made special rigging for at least three of the *Shamrocks.*

Bar steel shrouds had been used in the Twelve Metres *Tomahawk* and *Flica II* in 1939, but I am told that these were not cold rolled. The challenger's jumper stays, runners, and single forestay were all 1 × 19 strand wire.

I had not seen the challenger for over a month when I went into the building shed a few days before she was launched. I had met Sam Brooks, who asked if I had seen the layout. From the look in his eye there was obviously something very special about it. Climbing to deck level I was astonished to find that *Sceptre*'s layout really was that of an enormous Six Metre. There were two cockpits, the smaller one, right aft, was divided into two for the helmsman and navigator, while an enormous space just forward of the helm was for the crew.

It was this large cockpit which would have the advantage of keeping the crew hidden away when not wanted, with their weight about three feet lower than if they had been lying on the open deck. The weight of the enormous two speed reversing genoa sheet winches, which had been made as a gift to the project by Leyland Motors, was also brought well down. It would also give the crew a wonderful feeling of security, working inside the hull, rather than balanced precariously on the yacht's heeling, heaving, slippery deck. There was an enormous bilge pump at the after end of the cockpit, or 'bear pit', as it was christened by *Yachts and Yachting*, just in case she shipped a green sea into it. There was a hatch in the cockpit floor leading below, so that the spinnaker could, if necessary, be bundled down it out of the way. There was crouching headroom underneath, giving room for a small man to cook and to visit 'Blake' in comfort.

Naturally such a feature was still a fairly closely guarded secret, so that a jolly little game of cat and mouse was played with anyone suspected of being an American 'spy'. There was still the chance of the Americans copying it, if they thought it worth while. In fact, when they did discover it from photographs, they were slightly incredulous. At least one yachting journal contained a thinly-veiled threat to the effect that it was 'rule cheating' and that therefore the British could no longer complain of any American efforts to circumvent the class rules. This, coupled with the fact that of their three new boats that nearest the water was about two months behind *Sceptre*, tended to put us One Up in the nerve battle, which is all part of any *America*'s Cup series. One observer did comment that the possibility of shipping a green sea could not be overlooked, while another questioned whether the windage of a vast gaping space would help at all.

At first sight it did give the impression of infringing the spirit of the rules at least, but the accommodation required by them seemed to fit in quite neatly. It certainly satisfied the Royal Yachting Association's Official Measurers, T. John Black, William M. Smith, and Captain C. N. E. Currey, C.B.E., R.N. (Retd.), who signed her measurement certificate.

The finishing touches to any yacht, or ship, however large or small, always tend to be feverish. The weather was cold, easterly, and miserable, which made painting difficult.

There were three requirements for the outside coating of the hull. The finish had to be hard, smooth, and capable of being polished to a first-class racing surface, or as smooth as a bath. It had to look and remain good after prolonged exposure to the weather. It had to keep out the water, so that the hull would not soak it up and gain weight. Cellon had carried out various tests on bottom compounds and old-timers may be horrified to learn that the worst for soaking up water was the traditional coating, known as Black Varnish. They recommended their new Cerrux plastic sheathing, which had been under development for the past three years. This coating, which is formed by the interaction of a synthetic resin and a catalyst, is available in the forms of varnish, aluminium primer, undercoat, enamel, and filler, all of which are best put on with a spray.

To keep moisture out of the wood the inside as well as the outside of the hull had to be coated. The former was given a thin priming coat, followed by three coats of clear plastic. All this was brushed on as were the coatings on the deck brightwork

It had been decided to paint the outside of the hull white, with a scarlet boot-top, the colours of the Royal Yacht Squadron burgee. The finishing scheme consisted of first a thin priming coat of clear plastic, followed in turn by plastic aluminium, plastic stopper, undercoat, and then enamel. The boot top was applied with a brush to avoid masking. The priming coat on the lead keel was a special preparation to make sure that the other coats stuck to it.

The time available for painting and varnishing was all too short and the weather conditions were anything but ideal. George Robertson shook his head at one stage and asked that well-known Dragon sailor Duggie Tomkins, of Cellon, who was supervising:

'Has your paint cured or has it frozen?'

The last minute rush continued in the best traditions. The mast arrived on 29th March from Gosport, on the lorry which usually takes the Queen and Prince Philip's Dragon, *Bluebottle*, all over Europe. It was soon assembled by Jack Walford and Vic Nicholson. The latter regaled Sam Brooks with tales of what he had told Sopwith, when he lost two masts from *Endeavour II* in 1936.

On Monday afternoon, 31st March, the doors of the building shed were opened. A few elderly men, working with the leisured air of the highly skilled, had lowered *Sceptre* on to the launching cradle, which they had patiently moved in underneath her. They then eased her, very gently, out into the open air for the first time. As she lay on the fine transverse railway, which is a feature of the yard, David Boyd looked at her and remarked with a grin:

'She looks like a porpoise about to dive.'

This was no doubt prompted by the odd effect of the fairly heavy camber on the deck, in way of the mast, which was designed to put the sail plan the full eighty-two feet maximum from the deck allowed by the class rules.

She was moved sideways and then down the slipway until she was under the derrick. The mast had been dressed and was all ready to be stepped. The wind had been strong that day and it was getting late. The derrick was beginning to take the weight, but David Boyd looked at his watch and then at the sky. 'No,' he said, 'it's too late. We'll have it in first thing in the morning.' A canny man, Boyd.

The members of the Syndicate, who were attending the launching, began to arrive and to admire their lovely vessel.

The Commodore of the Royal Yacht Squadron, Sir Ralph Gore, a very great helmsman of his day, whose wife was to perform the launching ceremony, looked at her critically. He must have thought a lot. Perhaps it was of the old days, thirty years before, when he was the best helmsman in the British Six Metre team which beat the Americans for the last time in the British–American Cup races. Maybe it was also of the two *Endeavours*. He was British observer in *Rainbow*, when she beat Sir Thomas Sopwith's first challenger, and he was tactician in *Endeavour II*, outclassed by *Ranger*.

The weather was still cold on the morning of the 2nd April, but the sun was shining as it only can on a fine Clyde day. *Sceptre* lay gleaming. The signal flags, as some wag pointed out to the *Daily Telegraph*, spelt 'Good Luck *Scepter*'. All remarked on the beauty of her lines and on the golden sceptre, carved at the forward end of her gold caveta line. It was designed by Jim Macaulay, a ubiquitous, bearded figure who was one of Boyd's backroom boys.

The members of the Syndicate present were Hugh Goodson, Viscount Runciman, Viscount Camrose, Sir Peter Hoare, Bertram Currie, Colonel A. W. Acland, and Charles Wainman. Soon after ten o'clock Lady Gore christened her in the traditional manner and the seventeenth challenger moved very sedately towards the loch, to the spontaneous cheers of the large crowd who had gathered to watch her. She eventually reached the water, curtsied gently and was turned with the sun to be towed to her mooring. Boyd was there at the end of the jetty to see how she floated, an anxious moment in the life of any designer. He need not have worried. She was just right.

Those concerned with the building and honoured guests retired to the building shed, where Donald Edgar and his assistants dispensed the largest drams seen in Sandbank for many a day. The yard took a day's holiday.

George Robertson, in his speech, welcomed Sir Ralph and Lady Gore and thanked the members of the Syndicate for their generous and big-hearted gesture in financing the building of the yacht. He added:

'This is the most glorious day in the history of the yard, but we all look forward to a more glorious occasion, when *Sceptre* brings home the Cup.'

Lady Gore was presented with a gold bar brooch, similar to the sceptre on the bow, in a box carved from the yacht's timber.

Sir Ralph Gore, in reply on behalf of Lady Gore and himself, recalled the happy days he had spent racing on the Clyde, and congratulated the Syndicate on their fine and sporting effort, wishing them every success. There were further speeches in the same vein at the luncheon which followed. Hugh Goodson recalled the beginnings of the project and Viscount Runciman toasted the challenger with the words:

'We have all seen *Sceptre*, and you who wish her well will find better words in your hearts than I shall ever find on my lips.'

The next two days were miserable and a gale did not help the yard, who were anxious to put the finishing touches to her as quickly as possible. The smaller winches had been delayed, but were soon fitted in their positions round the large cockpit, for working the runners, mainsheet, halyards, spinnaker boom lift and downhaul. There was a certain amount of adjustment required on the rigging and the finishing touches to be put to the accommodation, which was also plastic coated, this time by Scottish Paints.

Sceptre certainly acquired a reputation early in her life for choosing the weather. At lunchtime on 11th April the flat ringing noise of a halyard against a metal mast proclaimed that she was being prepared for sea. The sun shone brilliantly out of a cloudless sky, while the light breeze gave the most perfect conditions for the maiden sail of the most photographed British yacht of 1958.

VII

Trials and Tribulations

IT was twenty-two years since an *America*'s Cup challenger had sailed in British waters and many had forgotten, if indeed they had ever realized, what a great interest was taken in such a vessel by the Press. A mistake had been made in indicating that the deck layout of *Sceptre* was 'secret'. Such a thing is always a challenge to the average press reporter, who will either find out the nature of the secret very quickly or make an intelligent guess as to its nature.

As Mr. Goodson stepped aboard *Sceptre* for her first sail, on the afternoon of 11th April, she was surrounded by launches filled with press photographers, several of them from American publications, so that any hope of hiding the big cockpit from them had obviously gone. As it happened, the Americans were inclined to be doubtful as to its value.

The crew who sailed in *Sceptre* on these early trials were: Commander Sam Brooks, who had been appointed Sailing Master, Lieutenant Commanders Graham Mann, Joe Brooks, and S. A. Potter, Lieutenant Christopher Seal, J. C. Connell, with professionals Jim Slorance, Keith Musset, and Cecil Jupe. They had been selected as a result of the practice races in 1957. Hugh Goodson was at the helm for most of these trials, and David Boyd was with him. A few employees of Robertson's yard, Colin Ratsey, the sailmaker, and various others were taken along. There were usually too many on board for really efficient working of the ship, but it was all very interesting and enjoyable.

I was on board on the second day out, when the Herbulot spinnaker belonging to *Evaine* was hoisted. There had been some delay in getting under way, because adjustments had to be made to the tangs on the mast holding the runners. During this period George Llewellyn, who had accompanied Goodson on the car journey north from his home in Devon, got into the launch which had been chartered by a photographer from an American magazine. When he returned he remarked, 'That fellow has been promised £100 if he gets a photo of you with a spinnaker set'.

The immediate reaction among some of the crew was that they should not go out, but Goodson said, 'We may as well give them something to talk about in the New York Y.C.'

The spinnaker was therefore hoisted when *Sceptre* was barely clear of the Holy Loch. No doubt the photographer received his £100. He was just in time because that same spinnaker tore to ribbons the next day, when the photographers' launches, aeroplanes, and even the helicopter, which had shown interest in *Sceptre*'s first trials, had all disappeared, leaving William Yuile to get the photographs, which are shown between pages 100 and 101. The loss of the spinnaker was blamed inevitably on the crew while some of them blamed each other, and others the material with which it was made.

It was quite obvious even then that finding and training a crew was going to be a considerable problem. David Boyd had devised the cockpit layout to make crewing reasonably simple. This was also aided by his bright idea of different colours for the Terylene ropes. For instance the runner tails were red, spinnaker sheets yellow, halyard tails blue. All were supplied by the Gourock Ropework Company, but in spite of these aids there appeared to be a certain amount of chaos.

On 15th April Hugh Goodson announced that he was satisfied with the challenger and departed for the South. A few finishing touches were required and she had to be prepared for the six-hundred-mile voyage to Gosport. A canvas dodger was fitted over most of the main cockpit and a wooden cover was placed over that occupied by the navigator during racing.

Sam Brooks spent much of his time up the mast checking the rigging, so earning himself the nickname of 'Burgee'. One day he swore that it was snowing at the top, with sleet at the hounds and rain on deck!

There was considerable gloom in the Holy Loch at this time owing to the sad death by drowning of Lieutenant-Colonel Archie Macalpine-Downie of Appin. His Brixham trawler yacht *Servabo* lay at the next mooring to *Sceptre* and he was a popular figure in Sandbank.

Eventually all was ready, and on the afternoon of 26th April, *Sceptre* slipped from her mooring with J. Herbert Thom at the wheel, and sailed down the Holy Loch under trysail and No. 7 jib. Piper Sandy Macqueen played her out of the Loch and as she passed Hunter's Quay pier the Pipes and Drums of the 8th Battalion The Argyll and Sutherland Highlanders took over. Church bells and steamer whistles continued the farewell. The wind was strong and after a hard sail she anchored in Kames Bay, off Port Bannatyne to disembark Mr. Thom, the designer, and the piper.

Sam Brooks had originally planned to lie there for the night but on listening to the weather forecast at 5.50 p.m. he decided to press on immediately. The wind was then westerly but was expected to back to the south-west. It was essential to make as much westing as possible. *Sceptre* therefore sailed as soon as the crew had had a hot meal, so that they missed the celebration of the birth of a son and heir to the Marquess of Bute. She reached Dun Laoghaire at 2 p.m. on Sunday, 27th April, where the crew were entertained by the Royal St. George and Royal Irish Yacht Clubs. They had had a fast, but rather wet passage and welcomed the offer of beds ashore and the opportunity to dry the boat out.

Sailing at 9.45 on the Monday morning *Sceptre* passed down the Irish coast by the inshore route. Tuesday was spent becalmed off the entrance to the Bristol Channel so that the mainsail was set in place of the trysail. She passed the Longships at 7.15 on the Wednesday morning and the Lizard at

11 a.m. She then stood over towards the Channel Islands, before tacking about six miles N.W. of Roches Douvres, at 3.30 on Thursday morning. The Shambles was reached about twelve hours later and she then tacked up the Channel to the Needles. After hailing the Royal Yacht Squadron at 10 p.m. and saying 'good evening' to Stan Bishop, skipper of *Evaine*, she sailed slowly on with a failing wind against the tide, anchoring at 3.30 on the morning of Friday 2nd May off the Outer Spit Buoy, at the entrance to Portsmouth Harbour. The crew were up again at 6 a.m. and 'Gillie' Potter and Christopher Seal started to tow her into harbour with the dinghy, before Bill Diaper came out to help with Camper and Nicholson's launch. In spite of the early start and the tiring passage the crew were enthusiastic enough to take Colin Ratsey and others out from Gosport, that afternoon, to look at some new headsails.

On Saturday 3rd May she was hauled out on the slip at Gosport. After a month in the water the bottom needed cleaning, while various minor repairs were necessary after the trip South.

From the challenger we now turn to *Evaine*, which was to be her pacemaker during the tuning up period in this country. Her owner, Owen Aisher, had fitted her out early after a pretty extensive refit at Camper and Nicholson's Southampton yard. She was launched on the 6th and by 15th March was in sailing trim. The Syndicate had always been very much alive to the difficulty of finding the best possible crew for the challenger. It became obvious that the best sources of fit young men, who could spare the time, and whose employers could spare them, were the armed services.

The Admiralty co-operated whole-heartedly by sending out a Fleet Order calling for volunteers, reproduced below:

*Sports—America Cup Race, 1958—Naval Volunteers for Crew

(N.C.W. 1221/57.—3 Jan. 1958.)

> A few men, who must be of a high physical standard of fitness and possess considerable sailing experience, are required for training with a view to taking their place in the crew to represent Great Britain in the America Cup race in 1958.
>
> 2. Applications from officers and ratings with the required qualifications, giving particulars of age, weight and general sailing experience, should be forwarded through the Administrative Authority to the Admiralty as soon as possible.
>
> 3. The grant of special leave with pay for those selected to take their place in the crew will be governed by the conditions of Q.R. and A.I., Article 0920, and it is expected that they will be absent from duty for the period March to October, 1958, inclusive.

Secretaries of service and other yacht clubs also recommended suitable candidates. As a result of these efforts nearly seventy men were given a trial in *Evaine* between 15th March and 15th June, most of them before mid May.

There was a suggestion later in the Press that the Syndicate had not been 'democratic enough', whatever that may mean, in trying to find a suitable crew. Considering the time available and the relatively few men in this country who could afford to spend the whole summer sailing, the real error was probably in trying too many. I am quite sure that anyone in the country, who was really thought to be good enough, would have been given a trial. If he had not enough initiative to put himself forward, would he really have been a suitable candidate?

The usual crew trial routine was for *Evaine* to take seven or eight men out for the week-end, or sometimes twice that number, working in shifts. This explains the apparent overcrowding, which some, who had failed to realize what was going on, had much pleasure in criticizing. Each crew were given an easy day on Friday, in which to learn the gear, with a tougher day on Saturday and a really rigorous test on Sunday. After the week-end, which was sometimes all too short, a committee, which generally consisted of Owen Aisher, Commander Charles Grattan, D.S.C., R.N., and Stan Bishop went through the list. Each man was graded either, 'three star', for a certainty, 'two star', for a possible (some were given two-and-a-half), and the remainder were rejected. The committee was almost always unanimous. All but very few of those tried would have been welcome aboard the average offshore racer.

As can be seen there was a certain vagueness in the actual requirements, so that an awful lot of men were tried, who, although they were very good sailormen, were not really young, quick, or tough enough for a Cup challenger's crew. The fellow who paused to light his pipe aboard *Evaine* during one of the trial days is unlikely to forget it. Nor are those who found that sailing in a Twelve Metre in the cold of March or April tore their hands to ribbons.

On one of the very first trial days *Evaine*'s spinnaker halyard disappeared up the mast. Quick as a flash a young Able Seaman ran up the mainsail to retrieve it. Mr. Aisher was so impressed that he wrote to the Admiralty asking for the man for the whole season. He was even more delighted when he received an affirmative reply by return of post!

The original plan had been to rub down and repaint *Sceptre* immediately she arrived in the South. As there was some doubt about the availability of a berth under cover this was postponed until 19th May. There were therefore a few days in which she could practise in company with *Evaine*, before the latter also went in for a short refit and the replacement of her wooden mast by *Sceptre*'s spare aluminium alloy one.

It had been decided by the Syndicate that the next month or so should be spent in trials in the Solent area, for the selection of helmsman and crew and also for making sure that, as far as it is ever possible, the gear and sails were the best obtainable. Obviously this could best be done under racing conditions, although not much attention, at any rate by the Syndicate, was paid to the results of any short races which were held.

It was perhaps a pity that greater steps were not taken to make these intentions known to the Press. On 9th May the two Twelve Metres went out to practise at Spithead. The practice routine which was generally followed, was as follows: the motor launch *Psaropoula*, belonging to Charles Wainman, one of the Syndicate, was anchored in a convenient position about a cable from a navigation buoy, so forming a starting line, to give a windward start. *Psaropoula* and the two Twelves were equipped with R/T, so that although the customary flag signals were hoisted for the starts, guns were dispensed with, as the time was called over the air, usually by Lieutenant-Commander Derek Woods, D.S.C., R.N., who conducted operations.

A typical day consisted of four practice starts, each starting signal being the ten-minute signal for the next start. On the fourth start, there was often a short 'race' to a convenient mark to windward, and then back to the line. There might then be a pause for lunch and the routine was repeated, maybe with variations, in the afternoon. The starts themselves might follow a definite pattern, in order to test some particular tactic, or be a 'free for all' battle of wits between the helmsmen concerned. Graham Mann was helmsman of *Sceptre*, and to test him a variety of people were put into *Evaine*. On the challenger's first appearance, Lieutenant-Colonel R. S. G. Perry was at the helm of the older boat. As he had the better of the starts and the practice 'races' were very short (about a mile to windward and back), the challenger never had sufficient time to catch up. *Sceptre* fared better the next day and led in both races, but it was not until 11th May, when the two boats raced from Spithead to Cowes with *Sceptre* winning quite comfortably, that the challenger's great power was demonstrated. It must be remembered that during this week-end *Evaine* had her old mast and cotton sails, while the challenger had synthetic sails, although to minimize the effect of these she usually set a smaller headsail than the older boat. These small headsails were found at that stage to be of doubtful efficiency.

However, by then the critics were at work. It has long been the privilege of the more ancient mariners to criticize any new boat. Based as she was at Gosport, where the previous four challengers had been built, *Sceptre* certainly received her fair share of criticism. Her trial crew, which was not always the same each day, and which was composed mostly of relatively inexperienced amateurs, was closely watched, particularly when getting under way and picking up moorings. Some of the Press, who found it difficult to obtain information, inevitably listened to the critics in the Gosport taverns.

Evaine was dismasted off Seaview on Monday 12th May, owing to the failure of the port cap-shroud rigging screw. *Sceptre* therefore continued the crew training alone. She received a new Terylene mainsail from Ratsey and Lapthorn's Gosport loft, so that no longer did she sail with her boom cocked up in the air, as was her habit with the Dacron sail, which had been made the previous year for *Evaine* and which she used on her early trials. To add to her troubles the luff rope slides on the new mainsail tended to jam, so that this added to the difficulty of manœuvring her in the confines of Gosport Yacht Harbour.

Kaylena deputized for *Evaine* on 17th May. As the weather was a bit rough it was a very gallant gesture of Lieutenant-Colonel W. T. Towers-Clark, who was at her helm, to come out at all, with this twenty-nine-year-old boat and a scratch crew. The very presence of another boat does give a helmsman and crew that element of competition which is so essential for match race practice. On that day the well-known American yachtsman and journalist T. Carleton Mitchell was taken for a sail in *Sceptre*. As he had already been named as the navigator of *Weatherly*, one of the possible defenders, this caused consternation. He had asked to be allowed to go for a sail well before *Sceptre* was launched, and his request had eventually been granted on the understanding that the editor of *The Yachting World* should accompany him. The latter could not and Mitchell went alone. His trip was probably of considerable interest to him, but the exchange of views between him, Graham Mann, and the Brooks brothers was also extremely valuable to them.

Unfortunately the fact that an American journalist had been taken for a sail, when only two British ones had (and those somewhat unofficially) did not improve Press relations. The official Press Day was not held for another month, so that there was a definite sense of grievance in parts of Fleet Street.

Sceptre was hauled out at Gosport on 19th May for repainting. Her mast was unstepped for improvements to fittings. A main halyard locking device, or 'skyhook' was fitted and the lower tangs for the jumper stays were moved a few feet higher. The smaller winches, made by M. S. Gibb, were all stripped down for cleaning and the boat was painted out inside.

It was at this time that a reorganization was made in the management of the crew. In the early stages Sam Brooks was in charge of the boat as Sailing Master to relieve the trial helmsman of the worries of the day-to-day routine; leaving him to concentrate completely on his own particular problems. As he had proved his worth, Graham Mann, who had been at the helm for the racing practice, was then given complete command of the boat, while Sam Brooks reverted to his job as Technical Adviser. While he seldom sailed in the boat from then on, he was still able to visit her and to go aloft occasionally. He is one of those people who is never happier than when up the mast.

As already mentioned, *Evaine* was also up the slip for a short refit. The challenger's spare mast was stepped, with a slightly different rigging plan. 1 × 19 strand wire was used for the shrouds, which were rigged with two sets of cross-trees and one set of jumpers. It was thought that this would give greater support to the mast, which was valuable as the only spare.

Sceptre was relaunched on the Tuesday after Whitsun, 27th May, and Graham Mann continued the crew selection and training. He found a triangle of buoys off Bembridge, about a mile apart, and he sailed round and round them. On the downwind leg there was just enough time in which to hoist the spinnaker, get it drawing and hand it again, if the manœuvre was carried out smartly. It was wonderful practice.

Evaine was back in the water with her new mast on 30th May, and was ready for racing practice the following day, which was a Saturday. The two boats practised off Bembridge and it was remarked in *Evaine*'s log that they were well matched.

The wind was light and they both eventually ran down to Cowes with spinnakers set. *Evaine* hoisted her Herbulot, which had been repaired by Ratsey and Lapthorn's Gosport loft. Jean-Jacques Herbulot had come over for a conference at the time that this sail was being repaired and it was decided that he should make one spinnaker similar to *Evaine*'s for *Sceptre*, and also an even larger one. As the latter was by far the largest he had ever designed, it was decided that it would be made under his supervision at Gosport, a very generous and big-hearted gesture by Ratsey and Lapthorn's, and by Herbulot himself.

As *Sceptre* only had a small spinnaker borrowed from *Kaylena*, it was hardly surprising that she was outrun. That Saturday was a beautiful day and the populace who thronged the beaches watched the challenger being led by the older boat. They were told by many of the ancient mariner critics, who watched like vultures, that *Sceptre* was behind, and that she was no good.

On the Sunday the honours were shared, but only just, so that Monday was devoted to tuning trials on the wind. *Sceptre* moved weight aft, which seemed to improve her. Some of the more knowledgeable critics had remarked on how she tended to put her nose down, or 'root' as it is called, when going to windward. It was very difficult in the almost continual lop on the moorings in Cowes Roads, where both boats were based for the next fortnight, to sight the waterline marks to see if she was floating as designed, but all unnecessary weight was removed.

On the Wednesday, with Sir Thomas Sopwith at the helm, *Evaine* beat *Sceptre*, but Graham Mann had his revenge the next day. He put Sir Thomas over the starting line and also beat him handsomely. On the Friday the breeze was about eighteen knots and *Sceptre* really showed her pace to windward, although she lost on the two short broad reaches. This might have been due to lack of a kicking strap on her mainboom and also to bad sail trimming. There was a strong wind on the Saturday and both boats only spent a short time under way before returning to their moorings. It was publicly announced that afternoon that Graham Mann would be helmsman of *Sceptre* for the *America*'s Cup races.

Mann had been Sailing Master of the Queen and Prince Philip's Dragon, *Bluebottle*, in 1955 and 1956, winning the Bronze medal in the class at the Melbourne Olympic Games. He had come from the Swallow Class, as part owner of *Nortazo*, and was a fine example of how one, who was only considered a 'good average' helmsman, could transform himself to 'world class' with really concentrated practice. Some expressed doubts as to his ability in light weather, although it may be true that the ten-year-old *Bluebottle* was only really at her best in a good breeze. He was, at the age of thirty-four, considered young and tough enough to be able to stand up to the rigours of the tuning-up period with its continual post-mortems, and to the bally-hoo of the Cup series themselves. He was sometimes beaten on the starting line in practice, but was of such a temperament not to worry, and most important of all, his great charm helped in keeping the crew happy.

On Tuesday 3rd June *Columbia*, the first of the new American possible defenders, was launched. She was designed by Olin Stephens, the only man still living who had designed an International Twelve Metre, and had been built by Nevin's for a New York Yacht Club Syndicate consisting of Henry Sears, Gerard B. Lambert, Briggs Cunningham, William T. Moore, James A. Farrell Jr., and A. Howard Fuller. With her appearance and the apparently mediocre performance of *Sceptre*, as reported in the Press and by pessimistic visitors to the U.S.A., the attitude in the New York Y.C. tended to change from one of near panic to smug complacency.

Sceptre's racing practice continued on Sunday 8th June with *Evaine* again leading, mainly due to her superior performance downwind, *Sceptre* was the better on the Monday and in the evening she received a new large blue Ratsey spinnaker. She sailed better on the 10th June, but was beaten twice in a light wind by *Evaine* the following day. The latter was sailed by Graham Mann, who wanted to have a look at the challenger from the outside. He also wanted to see how he got on with Stan Bishop, as already it was becoming apparent to him that drastic measures would have to be taken if the challenger's crew was to be properly trained and that Bishop was the man to do it. *Sceptre* had been sailed by Colin Ratsey, but by then was beginning to be sluggish due to a dirty bottom.

Anyone who owns a keel boat racing in the Solent knows that unless the bottom is coated with some anti-fouling, or a hard racing copper finish, such as that used by *Evaine*, it is necessary to come out of the water at least every ten days. Bishop, who was skipper of Sir William Burton's *Marina* and then *Jenetta*, before the war, said that his owner always slipped once a week, for which the charge was £25. The skipper received 10/– from the yard concerned.

An anti-fouling polish had been applied to *Sceptre*'s bottom, but judging by the brown colour showing, instead of white, neither this polish nor attempts by frogmen to clean the bottom, had been very effective. In spite of this obvious impediment, and Graham Mann said that he never realized how bad it was, *Sceptre* still often went faster to windward than

Robert Auld (left) and Malcolm MacLachlan (right) laminating the cockpit coaming while in far rear Charles Sillars is fitting the margin plank round the cockpit. Mr. Wm. Robertson is seen in near background considering this operation which he photographed for I.T.V. showing

Duncan Barclay fits the fore hatch

James Hunter at work on the rudder heel of Sceptre

Sceptre's *deck after the seams had been paid*

Richard Murray carves the name on the transom

David Boyd has a last look over Sceptre *before she is hauled out of her building berth*

Sceptre *in the open for the first time*

Lady Gore christens Sceptre

Thirty seconds in the life of a spinnaker

1

2

3

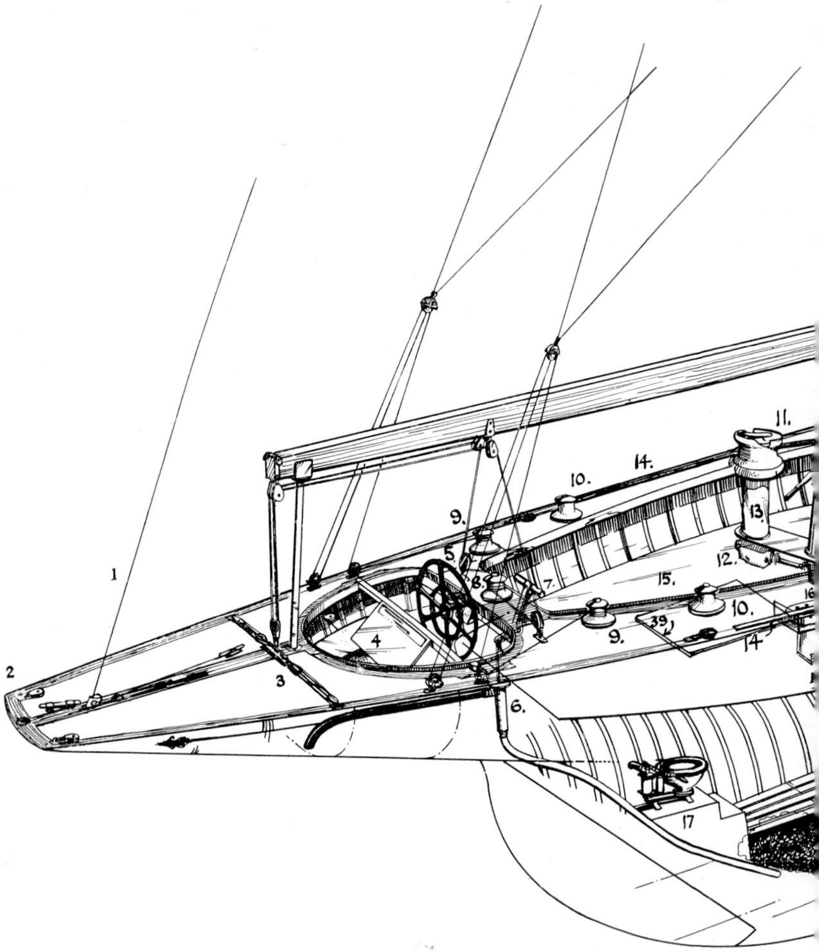
1
2
3
4
5
6.
7.
8.
9.
9.
10.
10.
11.
12.
13.
14.
14
15.
16
17
39

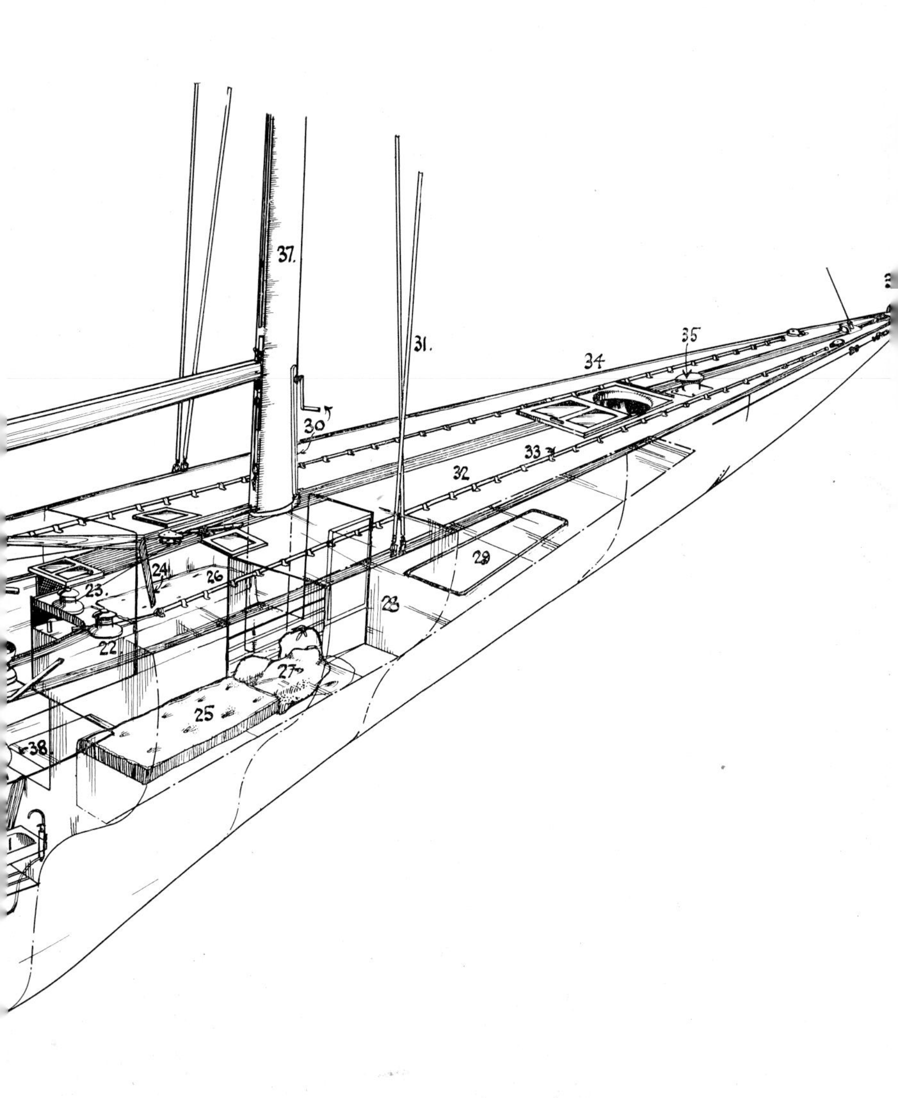

See key to numbers in Appendix F

Reeving Sceptre's *blue Terylene jib halyard tail*

Making one of Sceptre's *mainsails at Ratsey and Lapthorn's Gosport loft*

Hugh Goodson boards Sceptre *for her first sail*

Sceptre*'s foredeck*

The wheel and navigator's cockpit

Looking forward between the curved sides of the galley

Sceptre *and* Evaine

Colonel Perry at the helm of Evaine *with Owen Aisher*

Evaine, particularly if the wind speed was over ten knots. It was off the wind that *Evaine* so frequently passed the challenger but sometimes the wind was so light that neither boat would have completed the *America*'s Cup course within the time limit, which requires a speed made good of about four knots. In this phase of the programme there were really no proper races, as each practice 'race' lasted only as long as those concerned considered that it was still of value. They would then get into touch on R/T and agree to make another start. The period ended with two days on which *Evaine* was sailed by J. Herbert Thom. In the light winds which prevailed on the 14th and 15th June, he had little difficulty in beating *Sceptre* and in consequence a section of the Press blamed the poor performance of the challenger on Graham Mann. The latter even received a letter from an irate Scotsman suggesting that he should stand down in favour of Mr. Thom, who, at 67, was considered to be a little old for the helmsman of a challenger.

The second new American Twelve Metre was launched on 13th June. Her name was *Weatherly* and she was designed by Phil Rhodes and built by Luder's for a New Jersey Syndicate. The members were Henry D. Mercer, Cornelius Walsh, and Arnold D. Frese. Mr. Mercer had been inspired to form a syndicate to build a possible defender by a long friendship with the late Sir Thomas Lipton.

It was quite obvious that although a great deal had been achieved in the crew selection and training there was still much to be done. All was not entirely well with the challenger, but she was certainly not the dud boat which many critics labelled her. Various people gave vent to their opinions as to the reasons for her seemingly poor performance. The dirty bottom was blamed, as were the sails and the instruments, with which an attempt was being made to record her performance. The genoa sheet winches were not entirely satisfactory and had been a considerable handicap to her crew, but were being modified by Leyland Motors. The standing parts of the runners were too short. The wheel was said to be too big for light weather sailing and some said that the rudder was too small. Some criticized her heavy displacement and bluff entry, suggesting that the leading edge of the keel should be sharpened and that she should be lightened to allow more sail area.

It was all very interesting and at the 'post-mortems', which were held daily, red herrings were as common as bright ideas. Neither the Syndicate nor David Boyd allowed themselves to be stampeded into doing anything very drastic until they were sure that it was really necessary.

The question of sails was tackled whole-heartedly, as will be described in the next chapters. Perhaps the most encouraging feature of the week-end in which Herbert Thom sailed *Evaine* was the appearance in *Sceptre*'s afterguard of Frank John Murdoch. As already mentioned, he sailed in the two *Endeavours*, and in Sir Thomas Sopwith's Twelve Metre *Tomahawk*. He was also a very good Six Metre helmsman. He had acted as spokesman for the committee which chose *Sceptre*'s tank test model. He had also drawn the rough sketch, on the back of a menu card, on which the design of the genoa winches was based. His wise counsel and quiet approach was much appreciated. He came into the crew because Graham Mann and the Syndicate suggested that he should, and he readily agreed to do so.

The Press were allowed on board *Sceptre* on the 16th June and the following day she was slipped at Gosport for much needed bottom cleaning.

VIII

Tuning Up

THE two Twelve Metres raced from Cowes to Poole Bar Buoy on 20th June, *Sceptre* winning by 33 seconds, after spending most of the twenty-six miles astern of *Evaine*. The challenger's jib tack downhaul had parted on the way so that the delay in rectifying the defect handicapped her. The wind was fresh, and the fact that she won in the end was encouraging.

It had been decided that both boats should seek the rough water and heavy swell conditions to be found off Poole Harbour. A chance was also to be given to the challenger to sail with the same crew, at least for a month or so, to see how they shook down. Keith Beken, the well-known Cowes marine photographer, was in attendance with a ciné camera. He took several hundred feet of film of the challenger's crew in action and showed it to them a few days later, so that they could recognize their errors. Another feature of these trials were the analyses by the navigator, Joe Brooks, of each day's sailing. These were often merciless, sometimes tending to be libellous or verging on the obscene, but gave much ammunition for after-dinner discussion. They were posted on the notice-board of the Royal Motor Yacht Club and gave the members of that hospitable Club at Sandbanks, who were long-suffering enough to put up with the invasions of the crews for over a month, quite a lot of amusement.

Sceptre was at last fitted with a kicking strap, the standing part of the runners had been lengthened, there were rollers on the shrouds, and the two winches for the mainsheet, one either side, had been replaced by a single one placed amidships.

On 21st June there was a fresh wind, and after the customary few practice starts there was a short race. Lieutenant-Colonel Perry was at the helm of *Evaine* and he led the challenger over the starting line by 27 seconds. However he failed to cover her, and when he eventually did so *Sceptre* appeared to be sailing faster and pointing higher than her sparring partner. *Sceptre*'s winches had not been modified, so that she still tended to get the worst of short tacking duels, particularly in a breeze. Her crew often took over a minute to sheet the genoa home compared with fifteen to twenty seconds by *Evaine*.

On this particular day, after a three-mile beat, *Sceptre* led round the weather mark by 20 seconds. The hard weather spinnaker, recognized by a gold top, was hoisted quite smartly, and *Evaine* hoisted an identical sail, but made little impression on the challenger until the latter started to gybe the spinnaker. It was at this stage that Hamish Connell, with a lightning decision, jumped overboard to avoid the spinnaker boom which had taken charge and which might have injured him badly, if it had hit him.

He was picked up by Major H. W. Hall's *Ravahine* and when she came close to *Sceptre*, Graham Mann made him jump into the water before picking him up again. There was a reason for this apart from the undesirability of allowing the two boats to grind together in the choppy sea. A few days before, Hamish Connell and Charles de Selincourt had hoisted the spinnaker. When their task was completed Hamish turned to Charles and remarked: 'I've a good mind to jump overboard one day, when I've got a life-jacket on, just to see what happens.' Some of the crew thought that on this particular occasion he was carrying out his threat.

On Sunday 22nd June, the crew of *Sceptre* was as follows: Afterguard, Lieutenant-Commander Graham Mann, F. J. Murdoch, and Lieutenant-Commander Joe Brooks; Skipper Jim Slorance, with J. C. (Hamish) Connell, David Boyd Jr.,

Charles de Selincourt, Leading Seaman M. Tremlett, A.B. Tim Langford, Lieutenant Ian Lennox.

The crew of *Evaine* consisted of the owner, Owen Aisher, or whoever sailed as guest helmsman, Skipper Stanley Bishop, Commander Charles Grattan, with J. D. Sleightholme, Denis Jackson, Leading Seaman Tony Brooker, Lieutenant Ted Mappley, John Mew, Cecil Jupe, and Keith Musset. The latter spent a while on the sick list with a knee injury while John Mew soon dropped off the list to return to his dental practice. All the rest except Grattan and Sleightholme were to go to America with the challenger. George Wheatley was spare man, assisting Derek Woods in the all-important job of laying marks and conducting the races from *Psaropoula.* The name of this boat incidentally, is that of a Greek fisherman's wife and of a kind of caïque. It was in such a craft that Charles Wainman, her owner, escaped from Greece during the war.

With the crew more or less settled *Sceptre* undoubtedly began to improve, but there was still much to be done. With the delays in delivery of the spinnakers, particularly those of M. Herbulot, the gear had not yet been finalized, but was gradually improved with new quick-release clips and boom ends, while the boom was covered with film glass.

On Monday 23rd June *Sceptre* won twice with Colonel Perry at the helm. He had often sailed *Evaine* and was given the chance to try his hand at the helm of the challenger before he went off to sail the Royal Thames Y.C. syndicate Six Metre very successfully in Scandinavia. It was rather a pity that he left at this stage because there was no doubt that he is a first-class helmsman, particularly on the starting line and to windward, who often got the better of Graham Mann, so making him really work.

On 24th June *Evaine* broke her boom, which gave the challenger's crew a chance to carry out spinnaker drill on their own. One who watched them likened their efforts as equal to the crew of the worst boat in a rather inferior local handicap class!

By this time the challenger was beginning to collect quite a comprehensive locker full of sails. Two new mainsails, one from Ratsey and Lapthorn's of Gosport and one from their Cowes branch had arrived and were found to be very good. There was an ever-increasing collection of headsails, including two spinnaker staysails, and three spinnakers. On 28th June a fifth mainsail and a new genoa arrived from the well-known Californian sailmaker, Kenneth Watts. This was the result of a clamour in certain quarters that it was useless to contemplate racing in America with English sails.

It was quite amusing to watch people comparing the texture of the American Dacron sail and that of the newest light weather Terylene sail from Gosport. Few seemed to agree! Certainly relief was felt when the Watts mainsail was hoisted, because it appeared to suffer from much the same faults as the English mainsails. The genoa was certainly a beauty.

It was on the 28th June that the third new American Twelve Metre was launched. She was christened *Easterner*, designed by C. Raymond Hunt and built by James Groves at Marblehead for Chandler Hovey of Boston and his family.

This first phase of *Sceptre*'s working up at Poole ended with a race to the S.W. Shingles buoy on 1st July. Since 20th June thirteen races had been sailed. Of these *Sceptre* won eight and *Evaine* four, with one which *Sceptre* broke off when leading to practise by herself. *Evaine* had been sailed by her owner, Lieutenant-Colonel Perry, Commander John Stewart and C. A. Nicholson, as well as Graham Mann, on 23rd June, when Lieutenant-Colonel Perry sailed the challenger.

Sceptre was slipped at Camper and Nicholson's, Gosport, on Wednesday 2nd July for bottom cleaning and for modification to her genoa sheet winches. The gear ratios of these beautiful pieces of machinery were wrong and the gear change unsatisfactory, while the mechanism which allowed the sheet to be veered contributed unnecessary friction. Leyland Motors had remade the vital parts and were all ready to replace them.

Meanwhile the opportunity was taken to move them slightly further aft to give more room, when working the spinnaker. It also placed the drums nearer to the jib sheet leads.

The running battle over the instrumentation in the boat between David Boyd, the designer, and Navigator Joe Brooks was carried a stage further when the Five-Pen recorder, which had been installed to record the angle of keel, wind speed, speed through the water, apparent wind direction, and rudder angle was removed. It had required some pretty massive batteries, and the designer considered that the weight was superfluous. It was too late, in any case, to act on any of the conclusions reached, if indeed they could be relied upon. It was also felt that the absence of this rather complicated equipment would enable the navigator to concentrate solely upon his navigation. Joe Brooks and Ralph Vines of Thomas Walker's had worked hard on these instruments and their removal caused quite a rumpus. In fact it is believed that the rumour to the effect that Joe Brooks would not be the challenger's navigator originated at that time.

While this was going on another crisis was brewing. Graham Mann had felt for a long time that the crewing was not all that it should have been. Delightful fellow that he was, Jim Slorance was not really tough enough to rule the crew as a Cup challenger's should have been. *Sceptre* already had quite a reputation for being late in getting under way, and it was felt that the real answer was to ask Mr. Aisher to release his skipper, Stan Bishop, to the challenger.

There were some misgivings about this move because most people surmised that without Bishop in her to provide continuity, in a boat which was sailed by various different helmsmen, to prevent Mann from becoming too stereotyped, *Evaine* would no longer provide the really tough opposition which the challenger required. However Owen Aisher agreed that Bishop should join the challenger when *Evaine* had returned to Poole. Slorance resigned and behaved with considerable dignity over the whole affair, which must have been a bitter disappointment to him.

Sceptre came off the slip at Gosport early on Sunday morning and beat *Evaine* that afternoon, off Bembridge. In the light wind, and with her new red, white, and blue Herbulot spinnaker set, she ran away from *Evaine* with a similar sail. She returned to Poole on 7th July by herself.

On 9th July the party who were to go to Newport, Rhode Island, with *Sceptre*, together with the designer David Boyd and members of the Syndicate, were received by Prince Philip at Buckingham Palace. The Queen was ill at the time, so was unable to receive them herself as had been planned. David Boyd took along a model of the challenger, which had been made by the loftsman in Robertson's.

On 10th July *Sceptre* went out to meet and race against *Evaine*, which was being sailed down from the Hamble River by Franklyn Woodroffe. The challenger won, and Joe Brooks recorded that for the first time the spinnaker drill was flawless! Certainly the two foredeck hands, Connell and de Selincourt, were becoming pretty proficient, although the former, following his recent excursion over the side, had received a cut on his head which required four stitches.

Frank Murdoch was not available for the final phase of the racing in this country, but there is no doubt that his advice had helped an enormous lot. Almost from the day he joined there had been a steady improvement in *Sceptre*'s performance. Graham Mann remarked at the time how very sensitive the challenger was to even the smallest adjustment on the sheets, a characteristic common in Boyd's Six Metres. Even the slightest difference in tension of the runners made a difference in the helm carried on one tack to the other. Only gradually were these things discovered, as were the qualities of the sails. The three-mitre genoa, for instance, was much the best in a breeze, the No. 4 Gosport mainsail was the best in light weather as was the new Watts genoa. Some of these sails had to be nursed for fear of spoiling them before the Cup races.

Murdoch, in company with Stewart Morris and Peter Scott, had been appointed as an official observer to the Syndicate early in the summer. Their comments on handling and tactics were of the very greatest value.

Bishop joined *Sceptre* on 11th July and there was no doubt that his presence smartened up the crew. From the day *Sceptre* left Camper and Nicholson's, at Gosport, on 6th July, until she arrived at their Southampton yard on 27th, the two boats sailed twenty-three races, with *Evaine* winning only twice, although she claimed a moral victory on another occasion. Hugh Goodson was at her helm on 14th July, when she beat the challenger, and Jack Mellor beat her in one race a couple of days later. *Evaine*'s helm was also taken during this period by Captain J. H. Illingworth, Commander John Stewart, Robin Aisher, Peter Nicholson, and Sir Charles Taylor. The owner took her on the last day, 27th July, when they raced from Poole to Cowes, to give the Commodore and members of the Royal Yacht Squadron a chance to wish her good luck.

At the beginning of this period, and at the end of the previous one, the races were held well out to sea, to the Southward of Old Harry Rocks. The object was to get the crew accustomed to open water sailing and rough seas while the helmsman and navigator could work out their own particular problems out of sight of land. One snag was the use of free floating marks, which were not always satisfactory from the navigational aspect, as the tide was not constant in strength. It certainly made it very hard work for Derek Woods and George Wheatley, in *Psaropoula*, as she rolled like the devil.

As *Sceptre* was tending to beat *Evaine* very easily on the longer courses offshore, for the last ten days or so the races were held from a starting line in the vicinity of Poole Bar Buoy. An equilateral triangle, two miles a side, was laid with the first leg to windward. It was therefore possible to concentrate on crew training. The courses generally consisted of one round of the triangle and once to the windward mark and return. The crew were exercised on the points of sailing to be expected in the Cup races, but did not have much time to relax. The process was often repeated in the afternoon, unless some special trials were carried out. At times *Evaine* fared well enough. She often appeared to sail as fast through the water as the challenger, but the latter generally climbed out to weather on the beats. If *Sceptre* overstood the weather mark and eased sheets slightly she sometimes showed an astonishing turn of speed. This superiority was apparent in almost any weather, so that it was often necessary for Graham Mann to circle the leeward mark a few times to allow *Evaine* to catch up, or call a halt and start again. Sometimes the spinnaker team's efforts allowed *Evaine* to overhaul the challenger, but these occasions were becoming less frequent.

With the improvements to the genoa sheet winches *Evaine* could no longer rival her on a short tacking duel. It was taking an average of 12 to 15 seconds from the time when Graham Mann said, 'Lee oh!' to Bishop's 'That'll do boys,' as the genoa was sheeted home on the other tack.

The 'huge' Herbulot spinnaker, which had been made at Gosport, was delivered and tried. With an area of 5,570 square feet it was considered that it was about as large as could possibly be made, within the rules, which only governed the luff measurements. This sail was 92 feet on the foot, and it required a light cane bowsprit to prevent it falling under the bow. Obviously such a thing was kept secret and it was a discreet white in colour, rather than that of Herbulot's usual creations in the national colours of the boat concerned. It was during the trial of this great sail that Hamish Connell was again in the wars. The inner end of the spinnaker boom was attached to a sliding track on the mast. It was hoisted up and lowered down the mast by an arrangement of bicycle chains. The boom took charge when the chain missed a couple of sprockets, and the madly rotating handle caught poor Hamish. It was very painful.

Another secret weapon, a very flat reaching spinnaker, triangular in shape like a huge genoa, was tried in a series of pacing runs against *Evaine*, which had her Herbulot spinnaker set. It appeared to be a very useful sail indeed, more close winded than the Herbulot and it was put safely away in its bag.

Perhaps the most impressive thing about the challenger was the fact that she no longer dug her nose, but lifted it in the air, squatting on her counter. All possible weight had been removed and the spare sailbags had been stowed aft, in the tunnel under the cockpit, which can be seen in the perspective drawing between pages 100 and 101. The idea of stowing the spinnaker straight down through the hatch in the cockpit floor had been abandoned several weeks before. It was thrust into the saloon as it came down, and as the genoa winches had been moved aft, it no longer enveloped those who were working them. There is no doubt that with the proper trim the challenger looked a very much livelier boat.

Towards the end of the tuning up period in this country there appeared to be signs of staleness among the crew. This was hardly surprising as several of them had been sailing in *Evaine* in mid-March and had been hard at it ever since. Those of us who feel slightly jaded after a hard week's racing can probably understand. In spite of the obvious superiority of the challenger, *Evaine*'s crew, notably Charles Grattan, kept up a barrage of criticism, which certainly never allowed the *Sceptre* men to become swollen-headed. These critics were given the title of 'Antiseptics' very early in the Summer. The two boats had raced together on forty-three days, forty of them since 31st May, which was the equivalent of a pre-war season, compressed into two months instead of just over three.

Poole Harbour had proved an excellent place for the final phase of the training and tuning up. To a Twelve Metre, with a motor boat available for towage if necessary, the tides presented little difficulty. There was good accommodation in the Royal Motor Y.C. and in the hotels close by. There was a good slip at Poole and good workshops in the yard next door to the Royal Motor Y.C. The club itself was within fairly reasonable reach of London, and, more important, of the sail lofts at Gosport and Cowes and Camper and Nicholson's yards. Last but not least, there was the old problem of the Press. With everyone concentrated in a small area it was far easier for the pressmen, who sought information, to find it. In the earlier stages with the challenger at Gosport and *Evaine* at Cowes, it had been difficult to find the men really in charge. Even with both boats in Cowes it was difficult, and in both Gosport and Cowes there were plenty of arm-chair and other critics willing to give their often highly-coloured and sometimes quite inaccurate views, to anyone willing to listen.

There was no doubt that Owen Aisher, his splendid *Evaine*, and all who sailed in her, had done a wonderful job in giving the challenger the toughest working up that they possibly could. There had never, even in the difficult days in mid-June, been any question of *Evaine* being sent in place of *Sceptre*. It was always Owen Aisher's most sincere wish that she would be good enough to win the Cup. Of course, he did his best to show up the challenger's apparent weaknesses and criticized what he himself thought was wrong with her. Such criticism has always been part of the fun of yacht racing. The stalwarts who sailed in *Evaine*, like Stewart and Sleightholme, had no hope of sailing in the *America*'s Cup races, or even going to America. Those of *Evaine*'s crew who were, in fact, going over with the *Sceptre* party had little hope of finding their way into the challenger's crew, but they remained keen and cheerful.

For about the last three weeks in this country *Sceptre* had proved herself the faster boat of the two by about 13 seconds per mile, even in light weather. Whether this was due to the changing helmsmen in *Evaine,* or her loss of Bishop as skipper was anyone's guess. I believe that it was greatly to the credit of those who sailed the older boat that the margin was pretty consistent and was not greater.

It was rather sad on the wet gloomy afternoon of 27th July, to see those two lovely boats, which had raced together so hard, coming to rest off Camper and Nicholson's Southampton yard. *Evaine*'s light green hull, soon to have the challenger's spare mast removed from her, lay between two mooring buoys, while the white *Sceptre* grounded very gently in the mud off the end of the slipway. *Evaine* was said to be for sale, while the yard had a bare week in which to make the final preparations to *Sceptre* for her tremendous task.

IX

Some Problems of Ownership

THOSE who have even owned the smallest dinghy know that they have occasionally faced problems. Imagine then those which might confront the owners of the most elaborate and most publicized yacht in the United Kingdom, built solely to attempt to win the *America*'s Cup, the most elusive sporting trophy in the world.

It should perhaps be recalled that the challenge was first planned at the time when the Suez crisis was brewing and when the international situation was extremely tense. Even now it is difficult for a private individual to obtain enough dollars for a visit to the United States and though there were precedents for yachts taking part in events such as the British–American Cup and the Newport–Bermuda races, on the other side of the Atlantic, there had never been anything on the scale of an *America*'s Cup challenge since this country became short of dollars. The problems which confronted Lipton and Sopwith were infinitesimal compared with those of the early members of the Syndicate, whose first step was to obtain the blessing of the Cabinet for their venture, and in particular that of Mr. Harold Macmillan, who was Chancellor of the Exchequer at the time. This was given and since then the Treasury and the Bank of England gave all the help in their power, as did members of the Government, notably Mr. Alan Lennox-Boyd.

So far in this book I have tended to gloss over the work of the Syndicate. With a dozen members, it is obvious that some were more active than others, although all joined at one time or another in the periodic meetings, of which there were twenty-five, apart from the informal 'post-mortems', which were usually held after a day's sailing when Syndicate members were present. I asked Hugh Goodson's secretary, Miss Munford, how many letters she had typed about *Sceptre*. Her reply was, 'Thousands'. Sometimes she worked practically full time on the project, answering foreign Press queries, offers of help and all other matters.

The actual financial structure of the Syndicate is beyond the scope of this book. Suffice to say that the members were guided by the terms of a Declaration of Trust, by which the five most active members, Hugh Goodson, Major H. W. Hall, Sir Peter Hoare, Viscount Runciman, and Charles Wainman were appointed the managing trustees.

Ownership of a boat which is to be sailed by others is often a difficult business. It is easy enough to give those entrusted with her a free hand if things are going well, but if they are not it is always a problem to find the best remedy. The more active members of the Syndicate were in close touch with the crews of *Sceptre* and *Evaine* during the tuning up. Hugh Goodson sailed in both boats at times. Major Hall was an almost continual and very acute observer in his fine fast motor yacht *Ravahine*, which was *Sceptre*'s tender in the U.S.A. Charles Wainman was often on board *Psaropoula*, when he could spare the time from the City. Sir Peter Hoare, as can be imagined, was the treasurer. Other members watched the tuning up and offered advice, notably H. A. Andreae, whose fine motor yacht *Idalia* was often in attendance. There is no doubt that the Syndicate spared no pains to find the best crew and equipment for the challenger, and this was not always easy.

The New York Y.C., in their big-hearted way, had offered all the assistance which they could give in helping the Syndicate to obtain equipment which might not be available on this side of the Atlantic. However from the start the Syndicate were determined to use British equipment if this was at all possible. Only in the last resort was American gear used.

Inevitably during the course of the tuning up such gear was obtained, through the help of various friends of the Syndicate, notably John Millar, who had business interests in the States as well as a house at Newport. It was he who had arranged for *Sora III* to be available for the reconnaissance party in September 1957.

In finding the best possible British equipment the co-operation which the Syndicate received from all branches of industry was tremendous. The genoa winches, for instance, might well have been obtained from the U.S.A., but, at dinner one night in July 1957, at the Royal Yacht Squadron, Frank Murdoch recalled how he had devised a winch for one of the *Endeavours*, which was made principally from Ford motor parts. It was then that he made his rough sketch of the requirements for *Sceptre*'s winches, on a menu card. The mention of motor parts immediately suggested the motor manufacturing trade. Sir Henry Spurrier was a keen sailing man as well as the head of Leyland Motors, and so the big winches for *Sceptre* were made by his firm. As already mentioned they were not entirely satisfactory at first, and while they were being modified Sir Henry was taken for a sail. When he came ashore he remarked that while his firm had made a good winch, they still had to produce the best in the world. A week or two later the necessary modifications were made, with the result that *Sceptre*'s performance in short tacking could not be matched by *Evaine*. So it went on, whether it was the pursuit of suitable lubrication for Tufnol blocks and the winches themselves, or the testing of fittings, of which the strength was in doubt.

Many had remarked in the early stages of the project that they doubted if any yard in the country would be able to build the challenger quickly enough to give her a chance to tune up. There were inevitable slight delays in the early design stages and in the preparations for the tank tests, so that, at one time, the postponement of the challenge for a year was seriously considered. It was then that someone had the bright idea of forming the four designers into a technical sub-committee and while they were awaiting the result of the tank tests they were able to put their heads together to think of the problems of the supply of materials, particularly those which might be difficult to obtain. A stockpile was made of these and there is no doubt that without the whole-hearted and unselfish co-operation between the three unsuccessful designers and David Boyd his task of building the challenger on time might well have proved impossible.

Sails had always been a problem. With the very rapid advance in the use of synthetic materials it was naturally thought that the Americans would probably be ahead of us in their development. During 1957 every available sample of American sail material was analysed and it was found that the latest developments on that side of the Atlantic were within reach of our chemists, spinners, finishers, and weavers. Inevitably there were delays in delivery of materials, and snags, such as uneven bias stretch in the finished cloth, but all the time Imperial Chemical Industries acted as a highly efficient technical advisory and co-ordination service.

A Melinex coating had been tried in 1957 on a couple of sails, but was found not to be particularly satisfactory. Sheet Melinex itself was considered, as the ban on it by the I.Y.R.U. did not apply to the Cup races. After strength tests it was decided that it would be almost impossible to handle in the weights which would be required for a Twelve Metre.

The Syndicate heard through friends in America that some of the new Twelve Metres were using a form of genoa in which the flow of the sail could be adjusted by tension of the halyard. With only one forestay it was an obvious advantage to be able to flatten or increase the flow of a sail without changing it.

Although he had never seen one, Colin Ratsey wanted to try to make such a jib, but it was decided that if such a thing was found to be essential it would be better to obtain one in the U.S.A. Incidentally in the early days there had been much discussion on the possibility of unshipping the forestay, when the foresail was set, as is the practice in the Flying Dutchman class, but this was dismissed as too hazardous. Certainly the elimination of jib hanks would have improved efficiency, provided that the luff wire of the sail was strong enough.

When *Sceptre* left Southampton on board S.S. *Alsatia* she had no less than five mainsails, thirteen headsails, and eight spinnakers, of which one mainsail and two genoas were American, and two spinnakers were French. The Syndicate were still fully prepared to buy any other sails in the U.S.A., if they found out in time that the defender might have an advantage. The complete sail locker when the challenger left England is contained in Appendix E. Those who have recently received a sailmaker's bill can perhaps make a rough estimate of the cost. They will almost certainly be shattered.

I have already mentioned the crew trials, which were carried out by Owen Aisher in *Evaine*. Some tended to wonder why the names of the crew of *Sceptre* were not announced earlier than they were. The reason was simple. There was always the possibility that employers, who had given men leave to train as *Sceptre*'s crew, might not be so willing to do so if their employees were only sailing in the pacemaker. Obviously the crew chosen for *Sceptre* were given the chance to sail together for the last month or so of their training in England, but there had to be just a chance, albeit faint, that those sailing in *Evaine* might find their way into the challenger.

The Syndicate naturally paid the wages of the professionals, except for Bishop, who was still under contract to Owen Aisher, with whom he had sailed ever since the war. They also sometimes helped, with a modest subsidy, to pay the board and lodging of the chosen members of *Sceptre* and *Evaine*'s crew, who, being mostly young and impecunious, sometimes found themselves living in rather more expensive quarters than they would have chosen.

Many have discussed the choice of helmsman. Few probably realize that the Syndicate and their advisers considered practically every person who was at all well known in the yacht racing world. Every sailing district has its experts and if their ears were burning during the early days of the project they know the answer now. For some reason or another such people were rejected. Maybe they were too old, young, busy, or otherwise unsuitable.

The question of tuning up in the U.S.A. was one which received much thought. The cost of sending *Evaine*, in terms of freight alone, was prohibitive. There was also the question whether she would still really be a match for the challenger at the end of the tuning up on this side of the Atlantic. At one time the possibility of joining in the New York Y.C. cruise in August 1958 was seriously considered, but rejected on the grounds that it might be bad for the morale of the crew if *Sceptre* fared badly and disclose too much to the opposition if she did well. A rather worn out American Twelve called *Horizons* was offered to the Syndicate, but the cost of refitting her would have been too great. Eventually John S. Dickerson very generously offered to put his *Gleam* at the disposal of the Syndicate on the days on which she would not be required as pacemaker to any of the American Twelves battling for defence honours. As there was a series of their trials from 16th to 23rd August, followed by the final trials, 1st to 12th September, this fitted in admirably. She was a good boat which had tuned *Vim* up in 1957, and had been built in 1937 for Clinton Crane to his own design. Her hull had been tank tested, and although she still had a wooden mast, it was considered a very good one. For these trials the intention was to crew up *Gleam* with the spare men from *Sceptre* and a party of Canadians, led by Paul McLoughlin, the well-known International 14-foot dinghy sailor, who was runner up in the Prince of Wales Cup at Cowes, in 1958.

Relations with the Press have already been mentioned. At

one stage in the project the possibility of appointing a P.R.O. was seriously considered; in fact candidates were actually interviewed, but no one was given the job. In Lipton's day this office was probably unnecessary as the owner knew more about publicity than most. In the days of the *Endeavours* the 'J' class was always in the news because of King George V's ownership of *Britannia*, which raced in the class.

In these days when major sporting events are regarded in some quarters as public property there should obviously be someone, preferably sailing in, or close to the challenger, who could give simple direct answers to the Press if they sought information. This is essential if the owners and crew wish to guard themselves against irresponsible reporting, which may give away useful information to the opposition, pure fiction, or mere 'sour grapes' picked up in the nearest 'local'. Perhaps the most dangerous chap from the security point of view is the pundit reporting from a distance with the help of contact men. It is doubtful whether anyone will ever persuade the average Press photographer that the best action photographs of yachts and their crews are taken from outside, but the presence of launches close to a yacht racing can itself be very disturbing to the helmsman.

Cup challengers or defenders will always be news, and *Sceptre* did not receive particularly good treatment in her early life. The visit of Carleton Mitchell to her was part of the reason. This was rather earlier than the Syndicate had intended, but there had never been any question of keeping him off the challenger. Indeed a return visit had been planned, with Captain J. H. Illingworth, the leading British offshore racing skipper, as the caller on the four American defence candidates.

Lord Runciman, because of his shipping interests, had always been in charge of organizing the transport of *Sceptre*, her tenders and crew to the U.S.A. The challenger had an all too short refit at Camper and Nicholson's, Southampton, after she had arrived there on 27th July. A gale blew on the

28th, making it too risky to unstep the mast after Captain Currey and L. Jacobs had sighted the draught marks. She was therefore not slipped until Tuesday 29th for repainting of the hull, for which a bare two days was available. The hull showed the effect of a season's racing and it seemed a pity that a longer period had not been made available so that a more thorough job could have been made. The Syndicate had had to weigh the desirability of the last week's sailing and the lift in morale from beating a rather tired *Evaine*, against the appearance of the boat, which was worse than they realized.

A few modifications were made. The runners were given an extra running part, making four instead of three. Arrangements were made so that the heel of the mast could be moved if it was found necessary, and so that the mast partners could be made more flexible than the existing rigid aluminium alloy sleeve. The instruments which had been removed at Gosport were replaced, just in case there might be time to use them in America, and so to avoid the fuss of clearing them through the customs if they were sent separately.

Sceptre was relaunched on Saturday 2nd August, and on the following day she was taken round to Southampton docks to be loaded aboard S.S. *Alsatia*. The cradle was not level and did not fit properly, which caused three hours delay. Eventually she was safely stowed on the forward well deck. With her in this ship went her motor launch *Orb* and Major Hall's *Ravahine*. Derek Woods was in charge of the small party accompanying her, which consisted of Keith Musset, Cecil Jupe, and T. Eales, the skipper of *Ravahine*. *Alsatia* sailed slowly down the Solent, passing Cowes at 6 p.m. on the Sunday of the Week. She was dressed overall and as she practically hove to off the roads all yachtsmen present were able to bid her farewell and good luck, signalling by conventional means or merely blowing the horns of their motor-cars.

Graham Mann and Sam Brooks had sailed on the Friday in the French ship *Liberté*, with some of the crew, while the remainder followed the next Thursday in the *Queen Elizabeth*. Bishop took up the rear by air.

A large house at Jamestown, across the water from Newport, had been lent to the Syndicate by Mrs. Sydney Wright, and as mentioned before the shore arrangements were all under the most capable control of Tommy Beddington, with John Millar in charge of the purely social side. With the expedition under way at last, and the crews doubtless enjoying the few days of the transatlantic voyage, Hugh Goodson and his Syndicate were able to relax for a short while from the cares of ownership and gather strength for the ordeal ahead.

PART THREE

X

The America*'s Cup—Seventeenth Series*

SCEPTRE AT NEWPORT

SCEPTRE arrived in New York on 12th August and was unloaded the next day to be towed by Morans to Stamford, Connecticut. When the main body of the crew arrived in the *Queen Elizabeth* it was a very hot day. Even worse was the fact that all bars were closed until ten o'clock due to local elections. Her mast was stepped at Luders Yard and she was towed on to Newport by her tender *Ravahine*. She arrived at noon on Sunday 17th August, to the cheers of the crews of the four possible defenders to be received by the Knights of St. Columba, bagpipes and all.

Newport is at the southern end of Narragansett Bay, one of the finest natural harbours in the world. The town itself is on Aquidneck Island and in the days gone by was one of the fashionable holiday resorts on the American eastern seaboard. The millionaires' 'country cottages' and marble palaces on Bellevue Avenue and Ocean Drive are some of the most remarkable houses to be found anywhere in the world. Many of them had lain empty for years, but the Cup races proved an excellent excuse to live in them again, so that once more parties in the grand manner were thrown within their hospitable walls. The harbour is rocky with low-lying land, reminiscent of the west coast of Sweden. The Cup boats lay at moorings in Brenton's Cove off the Ida Lewis Yacht Club. This was on the starboard hand of the wide harbour entrance and quite close to it.

Ida Lewis, incidentally, was a lady who was the daughter

of the keeper of the lighthouse. She was perhaps the local equivalent of Grace Darling, and rescued some seventeen souls from the sea. She had no connexion with the Cavendish Hotel.

Sceptre's mast had slightly more rake than when she sailed in England, but according to one critic there was still not enough. Others said that it was raked too much. It had a variety of coinage under the heel for good luck. When first stepped it only had a threepenny piece given by Jim Slorance to William Cameron of Robertson's, much to the disgust of the latter.

Racing practice started with *Gleam*, which had had her engine replaced before the New York Yacht Club Cruise. She was therefore no match for the challenger, which had to tow wasps, fenders, and even a bucket to slow her down. She even used her engine, which was really quite useful, particularly short tacking. However, it was a pity that the challenger had never had any boat which could really extend her since *Evaine* had done so during June.

All this time *Sceptre*'s crew consisted of Graham Mann, (helmsman), Joe Brooks (navigator), Stanley Bishop, Hamish Connell, Mike Tremlett, Ian Lennox, David Boyd Jr., Tim Langford and Charles de Selincourt. Frank J. Murdoch had been expected to rejoin the crew as Assistant Helmsman and tactician, but in the meantime Colin Ratsey, who had sailed in *Sceptre* many times, generally went along to look at the sails, if he was not on his frequent trips to City Island with sails for modification. In due course, as Murdoch was not able to come for business reasons, Ratsey was asked by Hugh Goodson to take his place. It appeared from experience in the rather steep seas that it would be necessary to sail with eleven men instead of ten, as intended, and Denis Jackson was brought in as the eleventh during this training period. *Gleam* was sailed by Owen Aisher, who had taken her over from her owner Mahlon Dickerson. She had two paid hands who answered to the names of 'Bud' and 'Frenchy', and they were assisted by *Sceptre*'s spare crew, Ted Mappley, Tony Brooker, Cecil Jupe, and Keith Mussett.

'Bud' at times took the place of two antiseptics who sailed *Evaine*, with outspoken but not unkindly criticism. To one of *Sceptre*'s crew lent to him for the day and floundering on a strange foredeck he asked, 'Was you picked outa seventy guys?' 'Yes,' was the reply. 'Jees, what were the others like?' Hugh Goodson sometimes took the helm and Commander R. L. Hewitt, Sam Brooks and others lent a hand. There was a day when *Sceptre* was beaten fairly and squarely by *Gleam*, and one facetious crew member shouted across as they went to restart, 'Can we remove that bucket?' The Canadians who had been expected did not turn up, it is understood because of a misunderstanding about their real function in the organization. Some appeared during the races themselves.

The complete crew, together with Mr. and Mrs. Goodson and Sir Peter and Lady Hoare, lived in almost monastic seclusion at the house called Horsehead, Jamestown, situated on the southernmost tip of Connecticut Island. This was most kindly lent by Mrs. Sydney Wright. Tommy Beddington was in overall charge with Derek Woods helping with organizing boats and cars. The Syndicate members stayed in Newport itself. With the help of the fleet of motor boats, which included *Ravahine*, *Gypsy* lent by George Lander of the New York Yachting Club, two fine Ray Hunt fast launches lent by Mr. Asbrandtsen and George O'Day, *Sceptre*'s orb, and a rather terrifying rubber boat with an outboard, communications with the boat at Brenton's Cove and Newport itself were reasonably good. It was perhaps a little further from Warsash to Calshot than it was from Port Weatherall, where these boats were kept, to *Sceptre*'s mooring. This U.S. Naval establishment gave the most wonderful help, allowing *Sceptre*'s tenders to use their little harbour and giving them the use of a fine store for gear.

Cars were lent by the Rootes Group or by their representative at Stamford, Connecticut. Some were new Hillmans, while others were somewhat elderly. One was a Chevrolet van, which on one fine day Colin Ratsey drove down with a load of sails for slight modification at City Island. In the light-hearted, almost schoolboy, atmosphere pervading Horsehead someone thought of rearranging the number-plates of these vehicles so that the front did not tally with the back. This was spotted in Connecticut and Colin Ratsey was stopped by two State Troopers, guns and all. They appeared reluctant to allow him to continue to sully the fair highways of their State with this rather eccentric identification, and suggested that he took it back to Rhode Island. However the magic word *Sceptre* worked wonders and Colin was allowed to proceed, with a warning.

I joined him at City Island a day or two later for the return trip. The tyres were somewhat suspect and Ratsey's man did not appear particularly optimistic as to our chances of getting through. We waited until the day had cooled down, stopping for drinks and dinner with some hospitable friends at New Canaan. On the road once more we had hardly been going an hour when one of the tyres burst. We were on the main Connecticut Turnpike, and as we surveyed the damage enormous lorries thundered past rocking the van gently in their wake. It was a hundred yards to the nearest post office, and we rang for a taxi, abandoning the truck with a polite message to the police stuck to the windscreen. We hoped to get transport to the nearest hotel for the night, and return next morning. Unfortunately the taxi never showed up, on the pretext that he was unable to find us. This seemed unenterprising, as we were at the post office and next to Greens Farm station. After a couple of hours a State Trooper appeared, who called up a breakdown van, known in the United States by the picturesque title of a 'Wrecking Car'.

This arrived about half an hour later and changed the wheel, which we had been unable to do, having no tools of any sort. We then drove, escorted by the State Trooper, who had been delightfully helpful, as well as interested in *Sceptre*'s chances, to the Pequod Hotel. We were beaten by a short head for the last room by a man who kept us in agonizing suspense by inspecting the room with deliberation before he took it. We were then directed to Bridgeport, about seven miles away, where we found rooms in an hotel through which enormous freight trains seemed to rumble all night. Looking at my watch on turning in I found that it was three a.m., and exactly twelve hours since I had left the hospitable portals of the New York Yacht Club: that remarkable establishment where members talk about yachts, in contrast to some English equivalents.

In the morning we spent many precious dollars on new tyres and continued on our way. It was very hot, and as we crossed the fine bridge which connects Jamestown to the mainland we had another blow-out. A good samaritan came to our aid, so that we arrived at Horsehead at two p.m. Twenty-three hours for that trip must constitute a record in this age of the internal combustion engine. We therefore unfortunately missed the last day of the observation races, but were lucky to attend the cocktail party given by *Sceptre*'s crew to the American crews that night.

Sceptre continued crew drill alone, when the Americans were not holding trials, as it had been part of the bargain that *Gleam* should be available to *Vim* should she be wanted. It was interesting going out to watch with Sam Brooks in *Gypsy*. I remember one particular day when Hurricane 'Daisy' was deemed to be due within the next twenty-four hours. The wind in the harbour immediately outside was northerly and about fifteen knots. About three miles out to sea it shifted 180° and was about six knots southerly. The rather steep swell struck one at the time as unsuitable for *Sceptre*'s portly forward sections.

On our return from the *America*'s Cup buoy *Sceptre* appeared to be on her way up the bay. Hurricane moorings had been arranged for her and for *Weatherly* by the U.S. Navy in Melville's Cove, a small natural harbour about seven miles up. It had, I believe, been a P.T. boat base, but was full of the impedimenta of a mobile torpedo range. This was all securely attached to the shore, but one rather dreaded to think what might have happened had it broken adrift. *Columbia* and *Vim* remained on the slip in the Newport Shipyard with the wind, which barely reached fifty m.p.h., and the hurricane passed well to seaward, howling through their rigging.

Perhaps the most important man in Newport, certainly to yachtsmen, is John Flynn, the assistant manager of the Newport Shipyard. A tall, charming Irishman for whom boats are a ruling passion, his good-humoured help was sought by all. The Press seemed more or less to camp out in his office, while those of Twelve Metre organizations seemed to avail themselves of the use of his telephone and the assistance of his stenographer, and they cluttered up the limited parking space with their cars. He never seemed to worry.

On his arrival in New York Graham Mann had been subjected to a Press Conference and had acquitted himself extremely well. He did so again on a couple of occasions and I think that far from finding that a 'yachting writer is only a baseball writer with a white sweater' as declared by Red Smith of the New York *Herald Tribune*, most American yachting writers were sympathetic men who knew their business.

During the American trials there was always either *Ravahine* or *Gypsy* in pretty close attendance with Sam Brooks, John Illingworth, David Boyd, and others out to see what they could learn.

I have already mentioned the spinnaker gybing technique which *Sceptre*'s crew copied. Another technique which was also copied was that of changing jibs. All Twelve Metres nowadays have single forestays. In order to change headsails when on the wind without the loss of time, and the indignity of sailing bald-headed, it was necessary to hoist a flying jib. All that is required for this is a jib without hanks and a really strong halyard which is hauled taut by a strong winch. Once this is hoisted and broken out inside the headsail the latter can be changed at leisure. After every day of the American trials Owen Aisher would hold court in the Muenchinger King Hotel and ask all who had seen them, 'Well, what have we learned today?'

As a result of observations during the trials two new full-size genoas were made at Ratsye City Island, one eleven-ounce and the other ten-ounce cloth American weight. They were both beautiful sails.

There were various rumours and counter rumours concerning a change of trial horse for *Sceptre* from *Gleam* to some swifter craft. *Nereus* was offered in the late stages, but this was declined. There was a misunderstanding over an offer of the used *Weatherly* which had never in fact been offered, and a rumour to the effect that *Vim* was to be used was baseless. There was a feeling in the *Sceptre* camp that it would be far better to remain a dark horse, while others definitely thought that hotter competition would really be beneficial.

At one time it seemed possible that the weak part of the organization might be the crew. They settled in to their rather schoolboy-like life with what appeared to be mixed feelings. It is hard for any young man to keep on training for nearly six weeks, while others around him appeared to be enjoying themselves. Shortage of cash restricted most from breaking out, but the delightful hospitality of the neighbours of Horsehead, notably Mrs. Wright's daughter Anna Baker and her friends helped to relieve boredom. That the crew came through the whole series, and indeed the whole campaign, with great credit is due in very large measure to the wise leadership of Graham Mann and Stanley Bishop.

They certainly made a very fine impression on those who watched them at work in the shipyard and elsewhere. They all, as one remarked, 'looked like Vikings' with their hair bleached by long hours of sailing. They found their way into the hearts of many who saw them by the light-hearted way in which they went about their business, so that it was hardly surprising that *Sceptre*'s following was even stronger than expected. *Sceptre*'s crew had two most entertaining sailing matches with the Saunderstown Yacht Club. On the first occasion they were presented with what was described as a piece of 'Victorian bedroom china'. They returned the compliment the following week-end with one of *Sceptre*'s lifebelts.

Two men who were not in the crew but who fitted in as if they were, were Tim Melloy, of Leyland Motors who had come over to see that the genoa sheet winches worked, and Tom Barrett, who came with the launch lent by George O'Day. They practically became part of *Sceptre*, helping with all the day to day chores, and with cleaning her on her many excursions up the slip.

It was lucky that apart from the mishaps of the last race, there were few gear failures. One of the most fortunate was when the forestay fitting broke. It was the day of the last race between *Columbia* and *Vim*, and as we came ashore from the hospitable *Windigo*, *Sceptre* was on the slip with a gash on her stern from which the erring fitting had been dug out for repair. It was lucky that it broke in harbour when the runners had been tightened up for Hamish Connell to tape up the jigged end, and not while under way. The spare mast was in Newport but it would have been a complicated and unsatisfactory business shipping it.

The spare mast had presented quite a problem. It could not, for some reason connected with its construction, be parted and sent over in two lengths, as *Sceptre*'s had been sent to Sandbank before she was launched. It was laid on her deck for the tow to Luders at Stamford, but the problem arose what to do with it then? Derek Woods found the answer, sending it by road. Some of the streets of Newport are almost as narrow as those of Cowes, so he called on the Mayor, who enlisted the help of the police and fire brigade. The latter found a way into the naval base with their ladder extended to ninety feet, and there it was taken and, mercifully, was never needed.

As the day of the races approached, Newport grew more crowded. It had tended to be that way because of the visit of the President. The Viking Hotel in particular was packed with pressmen, and if Red Smith's crack about yachting writers is correct it appeared that a Washington correspondent was a political correspondent with golf clubs.

An addition to *Sceptre*'s equipment in the final stages of preparation for the race was a fathometer and echo sounder. This surprised some as the same type of instrument had been removed from *Columbia* during the whole period of the building, and tuning up of *Sceptre*'s 'instruments' had tended to become one of the chief whipping horses of the whole project. Armchair critics, yachtsmen, and others expressed their views loudly and even with violence, which could only have been based on ignorance and prejudice.

As Ralph Vanes of Thomas Walkers has pointed out, the anti-instrument attitude is curious and unsupportable.

There is nothing new in the application of scientific aids to sailing, and no sailor, fisherman, or pilot, would willingly set off without a single aid in the form of instruments. Those who trust the echo sounder and the D/F set have replaced the old school of fishermen who navigated by the 'smell of the mud'.

Hugh Goodson had always been well aware of the value of instruments in both tuning up a yacht and racing. His Twelve Metre *Flica* had been used by him for callibrator trials, and in co-operation with Yacht Tests Ltd., an ambitious programme of research was drawn up, which was cut short by the Second World War. In this connexion Fairey Aviation Ltd. carried out wind tunnel tests on a Twelve Metre.

Hugh Goodson investigated the formation of Yacht Test Ltd. and Commander Pore was its chairman. The directors were Sir Thomas Sopwith, Michael Mason (then Commodore

R.O.R.C.), Major Harold Hale, and Hugh Goodson. The technical advisers were Charles Nicholson, Alfred Mylue, and J. Laurent Giles, who acted as secretary. The primary object had been to provide similar facilities to those available at the Stevens Institute for testing sailing yacht models. As has already been recorded these facilities have now been provided more or less by the National Physical Laboratory and Saunders-Roe, largely through the efforts of the Yacht Research Council, the surprising demise of which has already been mentioned.

It had been hoped to analyse *Sceptre*'s performance with the aid of the five-pen recorder which has been discussed earlier. This was done to a certain extent, but maybe not enough now that the disastrous results of her races are known. Time, however, was short, and it was decided to dispense with this equipment in mid-June and to concentrate solely upon the navigational and other equipment required while actually racing. Although the recorder was taken to the U.S.A. it was not used there.

The navigational equipment was as follows:

(1) *Compasses*

(*a*) For the use of the helmsman. Two R.A.F. type grid steering compasses. One port and one starboard.

(*b*) Cyrosin compass operating on a north point indicator.

(*c*) Hand bearing compass for navigator.

(2) *Water speed*

(*a*) Pito type speed variation indicator provided by Smiths.

(*b*) Walker Knotmaster as a stand by and for distance run.

(3) *Wind Speed and Direction*

The short mast on the counter which had been much criticized was removed for the races.

There was a very sensitive mast-head vane which was greatly admired by many Americans.
(4) A small D/F set-cum-hand bearing compass was found to be most useful.

The measurement of *Sceptre* passed off without a hitch, but *Columbia* was found to be five hundred pounds heavy and this weight of ballast was removed more or less on the eve of the race, which proved wonderful ammunition for the rumour-mongers.

As the race day drew near the telegrams of good wishes began to roll in. There was one, 'Best of luck to you all,' from Prince Philip. Sir Thomas Sopwith wired Graham Mann, 'As one *America*'s Cup Challenger to another I wish you the very best of luck.' Yet another was sent by *Endeavour*'s amateur crew. Altogether about a hundred and fifty were received by the boat itself, while the individual crew members averaged at least a dozen each.

Newport filled. The vast spectator fleet assembled in the harbour. The hotels were packed tight. The Newport reading room, stronghold of Republicanism, opened its doors to all connected with *Sceptre*. The oldest men's club in New England, it boasts one of the finest collections of sporting prints that I have seen. Rumours were generated and sent flying round. There was much talk of the next challenger, and the betting on the eve of the race seemed to swing towards *Sceptre*. She certainly seemed to be popular favourite. The number of people who remarked, 'I'd sure like you British to win,' became almost embarrassing. Those who had seen the challenger out of the water seemed to differ in their opinion about her. One well-known yacht builder likened her to *Ranger*, others took one look and started to commiserate. David Boyd and Olin Stephens exchanged pleasantries. David Boyd was quoted as having said, 'She may be a dud,' which was rather unhappily prophetic.

Anyone who was anyone was to be found in the Newport

Shipyard looking at one or other of the boats hauled out, or at the other fine craft such as Carleton Mitchell's famous *Finisterre* secured alongside.

The day before the race I went with Owen Aisher and Ian Proctor to the site of Herreshoff's Yard at Bristol. Of the yard, alas, only a large shed remains, but the models made by the 'Wizard of Bristol' in designing his many wonderful yachts are still preserved by his son Sydney. It was his son who was sailing in *Columbia*. We saw Nat Herreshoff's instrument for taking offsets from the half models and his many inventions. A vane type steering gear for a model which he had produced in the nineties and various catamaran models which might have been older still. As we stood in this room among all the evidence of the life's work of a genius, Owen Aisher remarked with a smile, 'I can't do anything that looks like *Sceptre*.'

The official and unofficial dinners, dances, and other parties kept the members of the Syndicate and the Squadron busy at nights. The Ida Lewis Yacht Club held a dinner at the Clamlake Club, at which there was an *America*'s Cup draw, the tickets being auctioned. It was on the margin of the final race and the winning ticket was bought for nine hundred dollars by Dick Bertram, who had been in charge of *Vim*'s foredeck. His outlay brought him in six thousand.

He was helping C.B.S. on the flying bridge of the *Duane*, and during the last race, which *Columbia* had to win by over three metres, he approached and said, 'Hugh, I am rooting for *Columbia*; now you'll understand, won't you?'

There was a monumental cocktail party held by the New York Yacht Club at J. Nicholas Brown's residence on the eve of the race, and this was followed by a dinner organized by the Newport Branch of the English Speaking Union. This was at the Breakers, a palatial mansion at one time owned by the Vanderbilt family, and at present preserved as an ancient monument. It was in honour of the British and American contenders for the *America*'s Cup, and other distinguished

Americans and Britons visiting Newport for the races. The crews of both boats had gone to bed. Lewis Douglas was in the chair, and it was planned that there would be no formal speeches. However, most of the top table, including the British Ambassador, Sir Harold Caccia, rose to their feet, and addressed the Assembly mostly in the lighter vein. Mr. Douglas paid tribute to the sport of yachting, and read messages from President Eisenhower and the Duke of Edinburgh. Prince Philip wished everyone the best of luck, and Mr. Douglas remarked that he thought it was probably an understatement of his true sentiments!

Major H. W. Hale threatened to buy a $\frac{5}{8}''$ spanner to unscrew the Cup from its anchorage in the trophy room of the New York Yacht Club, and Mr. Goodson gave an erudite discourse on the translation of 'rooting for *Sceptre*', a current expression. Perhaps the sentiments of most American Yachtsmen were expressed in the shortest speech of the evening by Mr. H. S. Vanderbilt. He declared: 'We have kept the Cup for over a hundred years and I would like to see it go, so that we could go overseas to regain it.'

CHOOSING THE DEFENDER

The *America*'s Cup has long occupied a very special place in the hearts of seafaring Americans. When it was first put up 'for friendly competition' by the original owners of the schooner whose name it bears, the United States were gaining a supremacy in sail which they held until the sailing vessel ceased to be a sound commercial proposition. The Cup became something of a symbol of this supremacy. It also eventually became a fixture in the New York Yacht Club in the centre of a rather gloomy little room between the famous model room and the bar, surrounded by other trophies which include the Queen's Cup, which is the major Club trophy.

From the time that *Sceptre*'s crew and her various followers arrived in the States, until the races started, it was almost embarrassing to be told by many people that they wished the Seventeenth Challenger would win. Often this was inspired by the same sentiment that made them cheer *Vim* during the final trials, as she appeared to be the underdog, but more often it was a genuine desire to see the great benefit which would accrue to the sport of yachting from such a victory.

However there was no question of letting the Cup go, if indeed it had to, without a real struggle. It was also true that no American yachtsman wanted to go down in history as the man who lost it. The three new Twelve Metres which were built as possible defenders have already been mentioned. The fourth competitor for the honour of defending was *Vim*, that really wonderful boat designed by Olin Stephens with which Harold S. Vanderbilt swept the board in Britain in 1939. She had been completely refitted in 1957 winter by her owner, Captain John Matthews, who had spent that summer collecting and training a fit young crew. *Vim* started sailing in April 1958 and was tuned up by Mahlon Dickerson's *Gleam*, which later became *Sceptre*'s trial horse. Donald Matthews, son of the owner and Emil (Bus) Mosbacher Jr. were co-helmsmen, with the latter responsible for starts and windward work.

Columbia started sailing in June and her syndicate had the use of *Nereus*, a 1938 Stephens-designed Twelve Metre chartered from Stavros Niarchos. In her tuning-up races Columbia was sailed by Briggs Cunningham while Cornelius Shields often sailed *Nereus*. He was a veteran of sixty-three who had had heart trouble a couple of years before, but was just about the best available helmsman. He frequently beat *Columbia* in those early trials and one cannot help thinking that those who spent their time criticizing *Sceptre*, which was having her teething troubles too, might have been more profitably employed finding out more about the defender. As it was the Press criticism of *Sceptre* was read with interest in the *Columbia* camp where it was interpreted as a smokescreen, while her afterguard admitted that very much the same criticism could be made of the defender.

Weatherly and *Easterner* were both in the water too late to have a really thorough tuning-up before the proper racing began. The former was managed by her designer, Phil Rhodes, who was given a free hand to find the best possible skipper and crew. Arthur Knapp Jr. was given the helm. He had been the junior member of Vanderbilt's afterguard on *Ranger*, in charge of spinnakers, and was a noted helmsman in the International O.D.s in Long Island Sound, in which he had rivalled Mosbacher and Shields for top honours.

As can be imagined *Columbia* was designed as an improvement on *Vim*, the test tank suggesting that she would be about equal in performance in medium weather and better if the wind was light and in a good breeze. She seemed a more fully bodied boat than *Vim* with rather harder bilges. *Weatherly* at first sight reminded one of *Evaine*, while *Easterner* was the most unusual of the lot. Her designer, Ray Hunt, had given her a pronounced sheer, a fine overhanging bow, and a rather short counter. Looking at *Vim* out of the water on the slip next to *Sceptre* it was amusing to hear the pundits comparing the blunt forward end of the challenger's waterlines and keel to the sharpness of *Vim*; some seemed impressed, while others shook their heads sadly and started to commiserate long before the races even began.

Vim had her pre-war duralumin mast while that of *Columbia* was an extruded job made by the Fuller Brush Co., while those of the other two were made by Luders. *Columbia* and *Vim* had two cross-trees and a set of jumpers and it was interesting to note that they both discarded wire rigging for streamlined bars early in the season. *Weatherly* and *Easterner* both sported two spreaders and no jumpers, the former having started the season with a single spreader rig, which was not satisfactory. All had their coffee grinder genoa winches on deck and these were of much the same pattern as fitted in *Evaine*.

Proper racing in the Twelve Metres started with the Charles Francis Adams Trophy on 9th July, off Newport, when *Columbia* beat *Vim* by 46 seconds over a 21-mile course, with *Nereus* third. The wind was variable 8–15 knots. The other two boats were not ready until just before the preliminary trials, which started on 12th July and which were hardly much of a test. One wag reported that the only thing they proved was that *Weatherly* and *Easterner* were not ready for racing. On 13th, 14th, and 18th July the yachts were unable to finish within the time limit, while the race on 15th was postponed because of fog. I am indebted to Steve Cady of the Providence *Journal* for the results of those races which were completed and which are shown below. The boats were easily identifiable by their hulls, because *Vim* was white with a copper bottom paint, *Columbia* all white with a blue boot top, *Easterner* varnished topsides and white bottom, and *Weatherly* light blue with a copper-coloured bottom. The latter, an epoxide finish which had anti-fouling properties, was put on with a trowel and felt like marble. The crews wore distinctive uniforms, *Vim* blue jerseys and white shorts, *Weatherly* light blue, *Easterner* yellow shirts and *Columbia* blue shirts and shorts. *Sceptre*'s crew wore white overalls or blue Jaeger sailing suits.

PRELIMINARY TRIALS

Date	Wind	Course	Result	Margin
12th July	15–18 knots Steady	21 mile Windward/ leeward	*Vim* bt *Columbia*	1 min. 3 sec.
			Weatherly bt *Easterner*, which did not finish	
			Vim and *Weatherly* won starts	
16th July	15–20	21 W/L	*Columbia* bt *Vim*, *Easterner* 3rd. (3 starters)	2 min. 32 sec.
17th July	0–6	18 W/L	*Columbia* bt *Vim*, *Weatherly* 3rd. (3 starters)	1 min. 37 sec.
19th July	20–25	23 miles Triangle	*Vim* bt *Weatherly*	3 min. 56 sec.
			Columbia bt *Easterner*	6 min. 56 sec

Vim and *Weatherly* were considered to have shared the honours at the start and *Easterner* beat *Columbia*

These trials were followed by a break for further tuning and modification before the boats met again on the New York Yacht Club cruise, which started on 2nd August. Three of the races were on a triangular course while four others were passage events from port to port.

NEW YORK YACHT CLUB CRUISE

Date	Wind	Course	Result	Margin
2nd August	6–8 knots	37 miles passage	*Vim* bt *Weatherly, Columbia, Easterner, Nereus*	2 min. 14 sec.
3rd August	10–12	26 triangle	*Columbia* bt *Easterner, Weatherly, Vim*	0 min. 46 sec.
4th August	5–10	26 passage	*Vim* bt *Weatherly, Nereus, Easterner, Columbia*	3 min. 46 sec.
5th August	5–10 Fluky	24 passage	*Vim* bt *Easterner, Columbia, Weatherly, Nereus*	0 min. 41 sec.
7th August	15–20	25 passage	*Columbia* bt *Easterner, Vim, Weatherly, Nereus*	0 min. 33 sec.
8th August	20–25	31 triangle	*Vim* bt *Columbia, Weatherly, Easterner Nereus*	1 min. 5 sec.
9th August	10–20	21 triangle	*Vim* bt *Easterner, Columbia, Weatherly, Nereus*	0 min. 55 sec.

There was then another interval before the Observation Trials which began on 16th August. *Vim* had shown that she was a really serious candidate for the honour of defending the cup, in spite of her 19 years of age. These Observation Trials were held over an *America*'s Cup type course off Brenton Reef Light Vessel, which was not quite so far out to sea as the proper Cup race course. There was, therefore, quite a large spectator fleet often over a thousand strong.

OBSERVATION RACES

Date	Wind	Course	Result	Margin
16th August	8–10 knots Variable	14 miles Windward/ leeward	*Columbia* bt *Easterner* *Vim* bt *Weatherly* Starts to *Easterner* and *Weatherly*	4 min. 31 sec. 2 min. 23 sec.
17th August	12 knots	24 W/L	*Vim* bt *Columbia* *Weatherly* bt *Easterner* *Weatherly* won start, others even	0 min. 16 sec. 3 min. 39 sec.

Date	Wind	Course	Result	Margin
18th August	6–15 knots	14 triangle	*Columbia* bt *Weatherly*	1 min. 22 sec.
	Fluky		*Vim* bt *Easterner*	1 min. 01 sec.
			Starts to *Columbia* and *Vim*	
19th August	12–20 knots	24 W/L	*Weatherly* bt *Vim*	0 min. 26 sec.
	Fluky		*Columbia* bt *Easterner*	0 min. 47 sec.
			Easterner won start, others even	
20th August	8–10 knots	28 W/L	*Columbia* bt *Vim*	3 min. 41 sec.
			Weatherly bt *Easterner*	0 min. 23 sec.
			Vim won start, others even	
21st August	15 knots	24 W/L	*Weatherly* bt *Columbia*	0 min. 17 sec.
	Foggy		*Vim* bt *Easterner*	1 min. 36 sec.
			Starts to *Weatherly* and *Vim*	
22nd August	6–10 knots	27 triangle	*Weatherly* bt *Vim*	0 min. 51 sec.
			Columbia bt *Easterner*	2 min. 18 sec.
			Starts to *Vim* and *Easterner*	
23rd August	0–8 knots	24 W/L	*Vim* bt *Columbia*	4 min. 39 sec.
	Fluky		*Weatherly* bt Easterner	0 min. 07 sec.
			Starts to *Vim* and *Easterner*	

After this series the pundits got to work to try to analyse the performance of each boat, as far as they could. Briefly, *Columbia* was considered to be the fastest to windward and reaching, but invariably gave away the starts and was not good downwind, due mainly to rather ponderous spinnaker work. *Vim* was always good on the starting line; Mosbacher appearing to have a stopwatch built into his head. She had tried a flexible boom in two races, but without success. The legality of such a thing had been discussed with the Selection Committee, who had permitted them provided that nothing more than the normal yacht's gear, such as mainsheet, kicking strap, and boom vang was used to make it bend. Spinnaker drill was generally superb and she seemed to run and reach very well. Her sails were probably not as good as *Columbia*'s.

The starting of *Weatherly* had been good and she ran very fast, her crew's spinnaker drill being as good as *Vim*'s. However, her performance reaching was good but slightly suspect and she was not good to windward. *Easterner* often had the better of the starts, but Charles Hovey at the helm never seemed to be able to hold on to the advantage he had won. She seemed to show occasional flashes of great speed but was generally inconsistent. Her outfit of sails was not as comprehensive as those of other boats and many thought that her only hope would have been to put her designer Ray Hunt at the helm. In actual fact she was given some new sails, and 1,700 lbs of ballast was added before the final trials. Ballast was also added to *Weatherly* in an attempt to improve performance to windward, although many questioned the wisdom of this move when the boat had fared so well in the series which had just ended. The last-minute preparations were hampered by the possibility of Hurricane 'Daisy' hitting Newport, but each was eventually prepared for the final fight on which their very existence depended.

The final trials started on 1st September over the *America*'s Cup course, which is laid each day from a mark 9 miles S.S.E. from Brenton's Reef Light Vessel. The Selection Committee consisted of W. A. W. Stewart as Chairman, with H. S. Vanderbilt, C. F. Havermeyer, George Hinman, Luke S. Lockwood, Henry S. Morgan, and Commodore Burr Bartram. Mr. Stewart had acted in a similar capacity in 1934 and 1937.

The Race Committee consisted of John S. Dickerson Jr., E. Jared Bliss, Charles F. Morgan, F. Briggs Dalzell, Willis Fanning and Julian Roosevelt. They were stationed in the motor sailer *Nor' Easter* with Roosevelt in the tug which towed the marks. Twenty minutes before the start the course was signalled and the tug set off to lay the mark or marks, depending upon the course decided upon. For the sake of flexibility the Selection Committee had decided that they would not declare the pairings for the races until they had seen the conditions, nor would they signify whether the course was to be the triangle or windward-leeward until the last minute.

The Committee boat and the tug were in wireless touch with each other: exchanging such information as the time of rounding marks and remarks on spinnaker drill. On board *Nor' Easter* was a tape recorder, and Dickerson himself, who was on the starting line, took a photo of the starts and finishes.

They reported daily on return to harbour to the Selection Committee, who might ask the competitors for any explanation as to tactics. The Selection Committee made no mention of what they were looking for, apart from a defender, and said that they would give no explanation for any decisions they reached.

At midday on Monday 1st September, the wind was about 6–8 knots W.S.W. as *Vim* got the better of *Easterner* at the start, leaving the Boston boat in something of a muddle at the Committee boat end of the line. *Easterner* tacked onto port and *Vim* covered her, and both continued on that course for a long time, with *Vim* gradually eating up to windward of her opponent.

Meanwhile *Columbia* and *Weatherly* made a very sedate start, *Columbia* near the buoy and her opponent up to weather by the Committee boat. To remedy her hesitance at the starts Corny Shields had been given the helm, but at first his boat seemed bothered by the rather steep swell. One could not but help wondering how *Sceptre* would have fared in such conditions. We probably got the answer at the start of the first Cup race. However, she got going and soon tacked on to port. *Weatherly* on starboard rather surprisingly decided to tack for the safe leeward position when they converged. At first she appeared to be leebowing *Columbia*, but after about half an hour *Columbia* had eaten out to windward of her. One got the impression that *Weatherly* might have been sheeted in too tight, but Arthur Knapp has always sailed that way. When they both tacked for the mark there was about five lengths between them.

Vim rounded the first mark nearly three and a half minutes ahead of *Easterner*, but the Boston boat took advantage of some spinnaker trouble in *Vim*, during which Buddy Bombard was seen out on the end of her spinnaker boom. *Vim* was only nineteen seconds ahead at the lee mark, but unfortunately *Easterner* spoilt her chances of gaining her first victory by poor work after rounding, when she tacked before she was properly sheeted in and the weather jib sheet hung up on the mast. In all the American boats there seemed to be an awful clutter of winches round the mast, which had to be wrapped in a canvas bonnet, which was not always very effective. *Vim* sailed away from her rival to a lead of just over two minutes at the next weather mark, which she increased to 2 minutes 58 seconds at the finish, in spite of *Easterner* setting a big red, white, and blue spinnaker.

By the end of the race the wind had increased to about 14 knots which seemed to suit *Columbia*. She gradually sailed away from *Weatherly* to win by 4 minutes 5 seconds, and it appeared that the addition of ballast had made little difference to the blue boat's windward performance and had slowed her on the runs. Some of the spinnaker work had been pretty impressive.

Columbia and *Vim* exchanged opponents for the races on Tuesday 2nd September. The wind was 18 knots N.N.W., and once again they were to sail the windward-leeward course. *Vim* had a reef in her mainsail and started under *Weatherly*'s lee bow. Soon both tacked so that *Vim* was to windward and *Weatherly* had a clear wind. The latter was just over a minute astern at the weather mark and she reduced *Vim*'s lead on the first run. *Vim* had shaken out her reef on the first beat and *Weatherly* held on to her well during the second beat and at the beginning of the run home there was only a minute between them, with *Weatherly* in an attacking position astern. Both boats had set their spinnakers very smartly and *Weatherly* gradually closed the gap.

Then ensued the most fascinating gybing contest which I have ever watched. *Weatherly* had set off on a different gybe to *Vim*, forcing her to gybe to cover. This gybe was not executed as smartly as *Vim* usually did. The reason for this may well have been the presence of *Sceptre*'s tender *Ravahine*. The challenger was on the slip for painting and many of her crew were watching the American trials with great interest. It had been noticed that the crews of *Vim* and *Columbia* had perfected a gybing technique which is almost magical in its simplicity, and Hamish Connell in particular was very keen to see for himself how it was done. On this occasion *Vim* noticed *Ravahine* very close and gybed in a different manner and not very quickly.

However Connell had seen enough to enable *Sceptre* to adopt the same technique. Briefly this works as follows. On each clew of the spinnaker there is a wire which acts as the guy and a rope which is the sheet. On gybing the guy is released by the trip-line on the boom and the spinnaker flies up clear, usually higher than it has been setting. The outer end of the spinnaker boom is dipped under the forestay and is then clipped onto the wire which will be the guy, which has been led forward. A special clip had been attached to the spinnaker booms of *Vim* and *Columbia* for this purpose, although this is not entirely necessary. When the boom is clipped to the wire guy skilful handling of the guy and the spinnaker boom topping lift brings the boom end up in close proximity to the new tack of the sail. It looks dead easy and if done properly the spinnaker will hardly flutter.

The two boats gybed seven times in the last forty minutes of the race with Mosbacher skilfully keeping his opponent on his outside so that he had further to sail. It looked for a moment or two that *Weatherly* might break through, and as I was watching from Phil Rhodes's fine motor boat *Touché Too*, we were getting very excited, but Ed. Raymond, who was at the helm of *Weatherly*, just could not. *Vim* won by 17 seconds, and a rather gloomy boatload raced back to Brenton's Cove, as poor Phil was sure that with two successive defeats the writing must be on the wall for the fine boat which he had designed and managed.

Meanwhile *Columbia* and *Easterner* fought out a good race. The Boston boat had hung on well to be only 30 seconds astern at the weather mark. She lost about another half minute on the run, probably because *Columbia* set an enormous Watts spinnaker, said to be ninety feet in the foot. It looked like one of Monsieur Herbulot's creations, although it was cross cut. On the second beat Easterner again sailed well and seemed to benefit from the freeing puffs, but on the last run the defender ran away from her when the breeze dropped to about six knots, to win by just over two minutes.

On Wednesday 3rd September many expected *Vim* to be matched against *Columbia*, but once more it was a windward-leeward course with pairings as on the first day; *Columbia* against *Weatherly* and *Vim* and *Easterner*. The breeze was S.S.E. about 5–7 knots, and Corney Shields at the helm of *Columbia* started in the safe leeward position. He was never troubled by *Weatherly*, which was nearly three minutes behind at the weather mark. *Columbia*'s big spinnaker did not look at all happy on the first run, probably because it was too big for the weight of wind, but *Weatherly* tried a desperate gamble of sailing well to leeward of the lee mark in order to come to it at speed, but this did not pay.

Easterner made a good start after Charles Hovey and Bus Mosbacher had chased each other round in small circles on the starting line. There followed a splendid short tacking battle, which included a few false tacks, of which *Easterner* had the better. *Easterner* forced *Vim* to tack once more to clear her wind when she looked as if she could lay the mark, which *Easterner* rounded one minute and two seconds ahead.

Columbia meanwhile with her creamy 'defender cloth' mainsail, known to her crew as the 'Purple People-eater', was sailing as though driven by steam in the light going, and poor *Weatherly* hardly saw her, losing by 5 minutes 56 seconds.

Easterner and *Vim* continued their battle on the second round, but there came a fatal tack when the Boston boat did not cover her opponent and it was all over. *Vim* won by two and a half minutes.

When the boats had returned to harbour the Selection Committee informed all the crews that *Easterner* and *Weatherly* would not continue to race in the trials. This was indeed sad for the owners who had spent so much money and for the crews who had worked extremely hard. It was probably inevitable as neither had really been in the water long enough to do themselves justice. Time however was running out and the real struggle for the defence was obviously between *Columbia* and *Vim.*

The wind was about 14–18 knots on 4th September when these two boats started their splendid series of races, which were some of the best I had ever watched. *Vim* was ahead and to leeward at the gun and both tacked. Corney Shields appeared to me to make Mosbacher pinch his boat and then drove out clear to leeward. After about ten minutes' sailing it appeared that if he tacked he would clear *Vim* and after twenty minutes *Vim* looked badly beaten. Mosbacher tacked when just short of the lay line, but the weather jib sheet got hung up on the mast and she had to tack again. This stopped her badly and was caused by the clutter of winches on the mast. *Columbia* rounded with a lead of just under two minutes and then hoisted her big spinnaker with an hour glass twist in it. Rod Stephens and his men on the foredeck were able to clear this without difficulty and the lead increased by another 22 seconds by the time the lee mark was reached. *Columbia* gained more on the second beat and poor *Vim*'s crew made one of their rare spinnaker errors. They set it with a twist, had to lower it and set another in its place, which took them about seven minutes altogether. This lost her another minute or so. *Columbia* therefore won by 4 minutes 21 seconds, a pretty decisive margin.

Vim had her revenge the next day, over the triangular course. The wind was lighter, about 8–10 knots from the W.S.W. and Mosbacher got on Shields's tail as he sailed down the line on starboard tack, forcing him away from the line at the buoy end. Both tacked and *Vim* crossed late with *Columbia* safely in her wake. *Columbia* tacked to try to clear her wind but over came *Vim* on top of her. This time *Vim* kept firmly on *Columbia*'s weather and it appeared that in the lighter breeze Shields could not drive her clear. Both boats overstood the weather mark, *Columbia* very badly, rounding 69 seconds astern. She then started to gain after both had set spinnakers and by the time both were about half a mile from the mark she was only a length or so behind, and obviously trying for the inside berth at the mark. *Vim* handed her spinnaker and broke out a genoa. It was always a pleasure to watch this manœuvre as the stops on the genoa were only broken three-quarters of the way up until the head of the spinnaker was down clear of it.

Columbia held on to her spinnaker and very nearly got an overlap. In fact just as she was about to bear away under her rival's stern she surged forward and it is said that her bow passed under *Vim*'s counter as she lifted to a sea. Goodness knows what would have happened if *Columbia* had obtained an overlap with her spinnaker and *Vim* in a position to luff her. Mosbacher might have made the defender look very silly indeed. *Columbia* made very heavy weather of gybing the spinnaker because a clip hook came adrift from it. This lapse was greeted with derisive noises from the spectator fleet and she lost a couple of hundred yards before she had lowered the spinnaker, set the genoa and then rehoisted the spinnaker. She gained again, and did so very rapidly. The visibility was down to about three miles and when the finishing line appeared both boats seemed to be slightly to leeward of it with *Vim* furthest down. With only a mile to go there was only about a length of clear water between them, but *Vim* hung on grimly to her lead to win by 10 seconds amid a tumult of cheers, whistles and sirens from the spectators. Mr. Vanderbilt followed his usual custom of giving a very special wave from the deck of his fine motor sailer *Versatile* to the crew of his old boat.

Graham Mann, who had watched from *Sceptre*'s tender *Ravahine*, shouted across to me in the Coastguard launch which acted as combined course patrol and Press boat,

'Obviously a popular win'. It seemed that many favoured the older boat, which was putting up such a gallant fight.

There was no race on the Saturday owing to thick fog. The boats could hardly be seen from the Committee vessel in the murk, so that John S. Dickerson hoisted the twenty-four-hour postponement signal and returned to harbour. There was a spanking breeze on Sunday 7th September of about 18–20 knots from the S.W. *Vim* was reefed but shook it out just before the start. About a minute from the start both were sailing away from the line on port tack at the Committee boat end. *Columbia* was ahead of *Vim* and bore away to gybe, while *Vim* tacked. *Vim* therefore started slightly ahead and under *Columbia*'s lee bow. *Columbia* appeared to be pointing higher, and after about twenty minutes *Vim* tacked with *Columbia* covering her about five lengths clear. *Vim* tacked again, but *Columbia* waited to gain full way in the fairly big sea before covering.

The race was virtually over and when *Columbia* reached the first mark *Vim*'s spinnaker, which the crew were preparing for hoisting, appeared to be dragging in the water. She rounded 2 minutes 5 seconds astern, and when she hoisted it the halyard appeared to slip, so that there was some delay in getting it to draw properly. *Columbia* was drawn farther ahead by her big Watts spinnaker, which she lowered a couple of minutes before she reached the lee mark, sailing without a spinnaker or headsail set during that time.

After about five minutes on the wind *Columbia*'s jib fell down, as the pennant at the head of it broke. In sorting out the mess Rod Stephens went over the side, but was grabbed by one foot and hauled back on board. This and the delay in hoisting the jib again took about two minutes, but *Vim* was too far behind to gain any real benefit. *Columbia* was 2 minutes 20 seconds ahead at the weather mark the second time, and gained another couple of seconds on the run to the finish.

Many now thought it was all over, but the Selection Committee decided to give *Vim* another chance. One could not help suspecting that one very good reason for prolonging the trials was the rather ponderous efforts of *Columbia*'s crew, compared with that of *Vim*. The *Columbia* crew were a set of dedicated teetotallers who lived in a vast mansion rented by Briggs Cunningham, called Beechbound. It is understood that the wives found it rather lonely at cocktail time, although one husband had an occasional surreptitious beer.

On Monday 8th September the wind was westerly and the committee set the triangular course. Mosbacher got a lovely start in the safe leeward position, leebowed the defender, and when she tacked did so on top of her. The breeze was 12–15 knots, and, unlike the previous Thursday, it appeared that Mosbacher was determined to sail the boat with a 'good full'. The two boats sailed as though locked together with *Columbia* receiving occasional dirty wind. It appeared to us who were watching from that extremely well-found ship *Windigo*, owned by Walter Gubelmann, that *Columbia* must have been an astonishingly fast boat to survive such treatment and still hang on. At one stage *Vim* appeared to have trouble with her 'coffee grinder' or a hang-up with the jib and *Columbia* tacked immediately, only for *Vim* to tack on top of her. Maybe Mosbacher learned from this as the next few tacks were a bit slower and he seemed to be letting *Vim* drive off before sheeting in the genoa fully so that he remained on *Columbia*'s weather. Came the time that both could lay the mark *Columbia* took one more, a fatal error as she overstood, *Vim* left her to it and the older boat rounded a minute and ten seconds in front. On the first reach *Vim* continued to gain, maybe because her spinnaker was flatter than *Columbia*'s. On the next the wind dropped a little and *Columbia* appeared to gain a little, but she then dropped back as the tail end of a rain squall passed over. *Vim* crossed the finishing line 1 minute and 35 seconds ahead to more tumultuous applause and the customary salute from Mr. Vanderbilt.

On Tuesday 9th September the wind was W.S.W. about

12 knots at the start of the fifth race between these two splendid boats. *Vim* crossed the line in the safe leeward position leebowing *Columbia*, which had to tack to clear her wind. A short tacking duel ensued in which *Columbia* was kept safely behind. About the tenth tack *Vim*'s jib sheet hung up again on the mast and she had to tack once more to clear it. This gave *Columbia* a free wind at last. However, *Vim* caught her, and after taking *Columbia* to weather of the mark rounded about a length in front. She doubled this lead on the run and rounded the lee mark with *Columbia* on her tail. On the long board which followed, Briggs Cunningham gradually squeezed *Columbia* up to windward and ahead of her rival. She was helped perhaps by a windshift and by an increase in strength to about 16 knots, so that she was 1 minute 9 seconds ahead at the mark. On the run *Vim* tried to find more wind to the southward, but this did not pay off and she lost by 2 minutes 49 seconds.

The race the following day was cancelled due to heavy weather and W. A. W. Stewart, Chairman of the Selection Committee, took the opportunity to tell the Press that they were looking for the best performance of boat and crew in weather they could reasonably anticipate for the Cup races. This did not necessarily mean the boat with the most victories. He also pointed out that his committee had no power to change the crews of any boat, whose internal organization was entirely the business of the owner or owners concerned. This was particularly directed at a suggestion in various newspapers that Bus Mosbacher should be put at the helm of *Columbia*.

At the same time there was a question of the helmsmanship of the defender. Corny Shields was ordered to rest by his doctor and was not available to sail in her the next day. This was regarded by many as a vital race. If *Columbia* won she would be first to win four as in the Cup races themselves, but if *Vim* did so it would level the score.

Briggs Cunningham was at the helm of *Columbia* when she

and *Vim* reached the rendezvous at noon on 11th September, and Olin Stephens had rejoined her afterguard which he had left to make way for Shields. Starting manœuvres began and Cunningham was seen forcing Mosbacher away from the line with about three minutes to go. He surprised many by tacking when he was still fairly close to the Committee boat. *Vim* tacked too and *Columbia* proceeded to luff her the wrong side of the Committee boat, whereupon *Vim* tacked too and bore away gybing so that she came in to the line round the stern of it. Meanwhile *Columbia* sailed on round the bow of the Committee boat, bore away across the line and started with a clear wind under *Vim*'s lee bow. A short tacking duel ensued in which *Columbia* managed to keep ahead. The wind was N.N.W. about 15–18 knots and *Vim* had a smaller headsail which did not help her in the lulls. The puffs tended to veer on this beat and it was not long before *Columbia* picked up an enormous advantage from tacking to the northward and tacking again when headed. Both boats then seemed to abandon pure match-racing tactics and tack on the headers. *Vim* got the benefit of a shift and was put straight back 'into the ball-game' as it is known amongst American sailors. *Columbia* in turn received another lift and rounded the weather mark a minute ahead. *Vim* was quicker with her spinnaker, the red-topped favourite, and she gradually pulled up on *Columbia* which had set her Watts sail. This seemed to be too big, as it never really filled properly, and *Vim* caught and passed her to round the lee mark about 8 seconds ahead.

She sat on *Columbia*'s weather for much of the second beat and even within a mile of the mark was still ahead, but again a windshift helped *Columbia* and she rounded less than a boat's length clear. Both had spinnakers set in quick time, but both had trouble with the halyards, so that they were not fully hoisted. *Vim* appeared to be catching up, but *Columbia*, with a smaller spinnaker than that set in the first round, gradually drew ahead. She luffed a bit to the north of the finishing line to take advantage of the veering puffs, and kept her wind clear. She never really looked in danger, and crossed the line 12 seconds ahead, to be saluted by the spectator fleet. It was a great personal triumph for Briggs Cunningham as he won the start and this vital race.

It seemed obvious to all that the trials were over, and as soon as they returned to Brenton's Cove the Committee announced their decision that *Columbia* was to be the defender. They called on *Vim*'s crew to congratulate them on a 'fine job', and a really magnificent one it had been. One could not help feeling after the third race between the two that the ultimate result was not really in doubt, but that as well as giving *Vim* the best possible chance, the selectors must have borne in mind the wonderful benefit to *Columbia* of the really tough match-racing practice. It was this really hard racing almost up to the Cup races which has always been lacked by the challenger.

Columbia had a bare eight days in which to prepare for the Cup races themselves. She spent the first part of it on the slip and then had a couple of sails against *Weatherly*, as well as practice on her own. She was said to have collected a total of some thirty-three sails in her comprehensive locker, while her gear store looked like Aladdin's cave. Her professional Captain, Fred Lawton, a splendid character, who was practically square in shape, had amassed the most incredible amount of gear. Her crew, whose names can be seen in the list at the end of this chapter, were all men who had had plenty of experience in offshore racing, but they had lacked the sharpness required for really tough match racing. Much of the credit for the efficiency which they reached must go to *Vim*'s crew and to Fred Lawton. *Sceptre* had been sailing about well away from the Americans while these trials were going on, and while she had many supporters and admirers at Newport and elsewhere in the U.S.A., no one who watched these final trials could have had any illusions as to the magnitude of her task.

THE AMERICA'*S CUP—SEVENTEENTH SERIES*

THE *AMERICA*'S CUP RACES, 1958

THE FIRST RACE: 20TH SEPTEMBER

America's Cup fever was rampant as thousands of spectators poured into Newport on the eve of the first race. One inhabitant said he had never seen such a crowd since the Jazz Festival of a few months before, but hastened to add that he preferred the yachting enthusiasts. There is no doubt that the races attracted a vast amount of business to Newport. No doubt the Jazz Festival did too.

On the grey morning of 20th September, as we boarded the U.S. Coast Guard Cutter *William J. Duane*, the harbour was astir. There were yachts and other craft hurrying out to join the enormous fleet of craft of all shapes and sizes which was making its way out to the *America*'s Cup buoy, an orange and white chequered buoy, whose bell must have been very trying to the race committee, nine miles S.S.E. of Brenton's Reef Light Vessel. As we moved slowly down Narragansett Bay, *Sceptre* could be seen at her mooring in Brenton's Cove, with Stanley Bishop up the mast for a last-minute check-up. Innumerable craft were obviously full of *Sceptre* supporters. The sleek blue motor yacht *Vergemere* discreetly flew the Royal Yacht Squadron burgee at her yardarm, others had Union Jacks, or large white labels 'GO SCEPTRE GO', or optimistic words to that effect. One little grey launch sported an enormous Scottish Standard, but was not visible in the later stages of the day.

Sceptre and *Columbia* were towed out by their respective tenders *Ravahine* and *Chaperone*. The challenger was escorted by a formation of motor yachts from the Rhode Island Yacht Club and a brass-funnelled ex-Naval picket boat owned by John Millar, which bore the perhaps pretentious name *Maid of Honour*. It is understood that an explanatory brass plate was to be found on her main beam. When we arrived out at the rendezvous on board the *Duane* we counted over six hundred boats, but it is understood that the real figure was about fifteen hundred, eighteen aircraft, and a Naval blimp.

The sun started to peep through at ten-thirty and the wind was northerly, about 6–8 knots. Visibility was good and we watched as craft converged from all directions. The destroyer *Mitscher* with President and Mrs. Eisenhower on board passed quite close, which might have reminded the historians of the interest taken by Queen Victoria in the first race for the famous Cup. We hoped that the President would be able to see the second boat, as Queen Victoria's signalman is alleged not to have done, but he left at about 2 p.m. to play golf.

One watched the fleet of boats assembling with a certain amount of apprehension, wondering how on earth the coast-guard and the U.S. Navy were going to clear a path for the contestants, but at about midday the terrier-like, small coast-guard launches started to chase them out on each flank of the course. They were assembled in two long lines well clear of the first leg with destroyers, a Canadian frigate and the coast-guard cutters seemingly holding them back. The course, of 005° (magnetic) to the first mark, was signalled at twelve-ten and the tug, which was to act as the mark, proceeded on its way. The use of a tug as the mark had been agreed upon at the captains' meeting before the races started, because of the difficulty experienced during the trials of finding the dinghy which had been used

Both yachts hoisted mainsails and *Columbia* was seen to be setting her famous Defender cloth sail known as the 'Purple People-eater', its creamy colour making *Sceptre*'s white Terylene sail look ice-cold. The clearing of the course became frenzied, with hooters and loud hailers or 'full horns' being used to good effect. On the flying bridge of the *Duane* we were frequently almost blown off by the siren just behind us. In general the discipline of the spectator craft was excellent and the good humour displayed by the coast-guard in shepherding them was exemplary. *Duane* was actually the direct-

Columbia *leads* Vim *at the last mark in the final trial race* (Norris D. Hoyt)

Columbia *driving to windward* (Morris Rosenfeld)

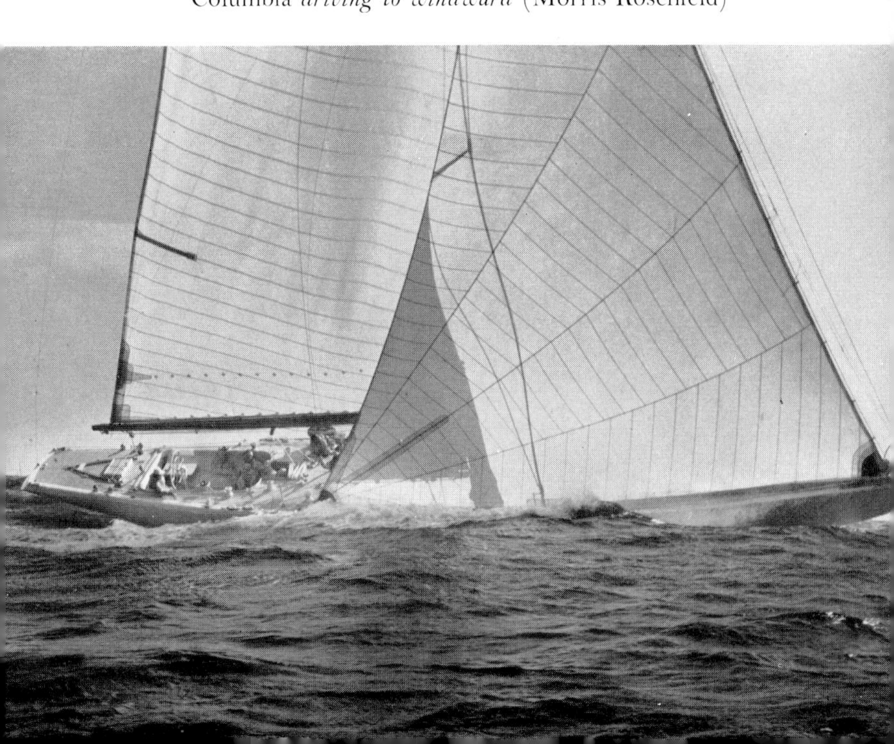

These photographs may tell the story of the seventeenth challenger. Sceptre's *round*

rward sections compared with the slimmer form of Columbia (Morris Rosenfeld)

Looking forward aboard Columbia
(Norris D. Hoyt)

Columbia*'s profile.* (*Compare with that of* Sceptre *between pp.* 100 *and* 101)
(Morris Rosenfeld)

Columbia *has broken through* Sceptre*'s lee a few minutes after the start of the third race* (Morris Rosenfeld)

A view of Columbia*'s deck* (Morris Rosenfeld)

Columbia *reaching, with 'Little Harry' set* (Morris Rosenfeld)

Sceptre, *twenty minutes after the start of the third race* (Beken and Son)

Columbia *thrashing to windward, using all her waterline* (Beken and Son)

Columbia *crossing ahead of* Sceptre (Morris Rosenfeld)

Activity on Columbia's *foredeck* (Morris Rosenfeld)

'A proper lash-up.' Sceptre's *main boom 'fished' with the spinnaker boom and boom crutch during the last race* (Morris Rosenfeld)

Columbia*'s crew:* (*l. to r.*) *Rod Stephens, Wally Tobin, Colin Ratsey, Jimmy Halsam, Halsey Herreshoff, C. 'Glit' Shields Jr., Victor Romagna, Olin Stephens, Henry Sears, Briggs Cunningham, Captain Fred Lawton* (Morris Rosenfeld)

Sceptre*'s crew:* (*l. to r.*) *Joe Brooks, Charles de Selincourt, Captain Stanley Bishop, David Boyd, C. Colin Ratsey, Mike Tremlett, Ian Lennox, Hamish Connell* (*yawning*), *Graham Mann, Tim Langford, Denis Jackson* (Morris Rosenfeld)

Columbia*'s crew giving* Sceptre *the 'big hand'* (Morris Rosenfeld)

'Well sailed, Columbia.*' The defender enters harbour* (Morris Rosenfeld)

ing ship and controlled the whole affair as well as looking after her immediate vicinity. At one stage there was a solid wall of small craft ahead of her but a call through the loud hailer of 'This boat weighs 2,700 tons and is going five knots,' soon cleared them!

The slight lop caused by the wash of many power boats together with the remains of a swell made conditions just about as bad as they could be for *Sceptre* with her full bow sections. The two boats made little attempt to engage in match race battle at the start, both apparently concentrating on trying to keep full way on. With about a minute and a half to go *Sceptre* was on starboard tack heading for the line. At one stage it looked as if she was stalling and was falling away badly, the lop knocking her back. *Columbia* was to weather of her and about thirty seconds before the gun bore away across the bows of the challenger on the same tack, rounding under her lee bow. Both boats were slightly late over the line, but *Columbia* with way on and a clear wind sailed straight away. A slight header put the challenger about a hundred yards almost dead astern of her within a very few minutes of the start, whereupon *Sceptre* tacked with *Columbia* on top of her. *Sceptre*'s jib had looked terrible, and it was changed extremely quickly, but she was already a badly beaten boat.

Sceptre was much stiffer than the defender and in consequence her mainsail particularly never seemed to stand at all well, shaken as it was by the bouncing of her rounded sections in the swell. A windshift made the first leg into a long and short board. *Columbia* tacked for the mark after sailing for about an hour and a quarter and rounded it while poor *Sceptre* had to tack twice more. She rounded 7 minutes 40 seconds astern and then a most remarkable thing happened. *Columbia* had set off on the run with her spinnaker set and drawing on the starboard gybe. *Sceptre* rounded and set her spinnaker, she found a private breeze, which seemed to be about the best of the day. She gained rapidly, and at one time was only about a couple of hundred yards astern, when both yachts seemed to be becalmed. As *Sceptre* had set *Evaine*'s Herbulot spinnaker many American pundits shook their heads and remarked that it must be too big for that weight of wind. It certainly was not, until the wind died, and the crew might have kept it drawing just a little longer but they appeared to allow the mainsail to kill it. At this stage *Columbia* had opened up a little, but had also lost the breeze.

The time was two thirty and it seemed quite possible that, following tradition, the first race of this series might not be completed within the time limit. However a gentle air came in and the Herbulot filled. *Columbia* had pulled ahead having set a 'ghoster', a very light headsail, but she then re-hoisted her spinnaker. At this stage *Sceptre* lowered her Herbulot and set a smaller spinnaker, the light white Ratsey, which looked very good. It was probably a mistake. Having held onto the Herbulot so long she might have persevered. Anyway after twenty minutes she set the red, white, and blue Herbulot in place of the white spinnaker and *Columbia* had changed to what appeared to be a very good reaching spinnaker. The wind by then was about 6 knots, and as they neared the *America*'s Cup buoy *Sceptre* lowered the Herbulot and set her genoa. *Columbia* rounded 2 minutes 20 seconds ahead of her, but as they set off on the second round it became pretty certain that the race could really only be a melancholy procession. The wind was then westerly, about 6 knots, so that it was merely a case of sailing two close reaches to the finish. On the first, *Sceptre*, being astern, seemed to luff to try to pick up more breeze to the west, but I suspect luffed into the dirty wind of the spectator fleet. This made no difference to the result, which was never in doubt, but one could not help noticing on seeing a bird's-eye view of the situation, that there was a vast area in between the two lines of boats in which the wind was being cut to pieces. There seemed to be a breeze to the east and to the west of these two lines but not in the middle. It was largely a matter of luck whether either contestant fell under a destroyer or coast-guard cutter whose wind shadow could extend 1,000 yards. There is no doubt that sailing an *America*'s Cup race in a very light wind does present its own very particular problems.

Joe Brooks advanced a theory that the exhaust gases from so many boats drove the air upwards, and this may be so. It is, however, just as bad for both boats, but may always be worse for the one which is behind simply because he tends to be hampered from doing 'the different thing', as required by the text-books on the sport. Anyway *Sceptre* lost a lot on that leg, rounding the third mark 8 minutes 15 seconds astern, but equally inexplicably gained a little so that at the finish she was 7 minutes 44 seconds astern, a pretty sound thrashing.

Times:	*Columbia*	5	13	50
	Sceptre	5	21	34
			7	44 margin.

There were some who said that the race was inconclusive, but they were probably either being sporting or tending to delude themselves, the defender had a win in her locker, and she had shown a very marked superiority in such conditions to windward. The only time that *Sceptre* looked dangerous was when she had a private wind. Her crew looked as if they had suffered somewhat from nerves, which was the natural result of the lack of really serious match-race practice. *Columbia*'s crew seemed to show better light weather sailing technique and her sails, her jibs, perhaps even more than the famous mainsail, were vastly superior and also looked much bigger than *Sceptre*'s. I consider that a win in light weather is often harder earned than one in a breeze, and this was a typical example.

AN ABORTIVE RACE: 22nd SEPTEMBER

Sunday 21st September was what is termed a 'lay-day' by American yachtsmen, so that there was time for *Columbia* to go up the slip. It had blown pretty hard during that day and even harder in the night, so that when we sallied forth on Monday morning there seemed a genuine hope of a better wind. It was about 12–13 knots as the *Duane* steamed out to the rendezvous, but although forecast from the south, it was actually from the north. The sun shone brightly and the spectator fleet was almost as big as that on Saturday.

The swell was from the south-east and the wind, as already stated northerly, but, alas, appeared to be dropping. It could not have been much more than 8 knots at the start, in which Graham Mann was in the safe leeward position. There was a windshift about the time of the gun, so that *Sceptre* only just pinched clear of the Committee boat, at the port end of the line with about four boats' widths to spare, and as he did so, *Columbia* sailed clean through her weather. They both continued on this course, many wondering why Mann did not tack when *Columbia* had opened out to some three hundred yards ahead. Both boats then lost the wind and *Columbia* was seen changing headsails. At twelve forty, twenty minutes after the start, the wind was completely flat and the sails of both boats slatted in the swell. One could see *Sceptre*'s racing flag describing complete circles, as she bounced gently. Soon there seemed to be more of a southerly tendency in this flag and at twelve forty-five, there was definitely a very light S.W. air. A few minutes later *Columbia* set a spinnaker, a small one with a blue top, but it did not help noticeably. *Sceptre's* genoa seemed to be pulling her well and she appeared to be closing up. In contrast to that of *Columbia* the challenger's mainsheet was fairly hard in and as her mainsail flapped in the swell it may have helped quite a bit in fanning the boat along. Perhaps this was our imagination. She seemed to gather way in a remarkable fashion and at five past one passed *Columbia* for the first time in the series. There was a terrific blast of hooters as she did so, which must have gladdened the hearts of Graham Mann and his crew, who were certainly looking more confident than on the previous day.

A few minutes later *Columbia* lowered her spinnaker and set her genoa, with *Sceptre* about three hundred yards ahead, she then changed jibs and began to move up, with her jib very noticeably bigger than *Sceptre*'s. At one fifty-three she set a white spinnaker. It was possible to see Joe Brooks in *Sceptre* watching the defender to see whether this move was paying off, and after nine minutes *Sceptre* hoisted the red, white, and blue Herbulot. The American pundits again shook their heads and said it was too big for the weight of wind, that the pole was cocked up too much, and the foot was dragging in the water. Both boats were well to windward of the mark, which was still about five miles away right inshore, but as they bore away for it, *Sceptre*'s lead obviously decreased. At two twenty-three both gybed on to starboard, and it was very difficult from the angle at which I watched to see the distance between them, but *Sceptre* seemed to be hanging on to her lead. The breeze was just strong enough to fill the Herbulot, and as long as it was there there was hope.

However, even at that stage it seemed most doubtful if the race would be finished within the time limit. About half an hour later both gybed again and *Columbia* seemed to be luffing across *Sceptre*'s stern to attack, but the slightly increased breeze kept the great coloured spinnaker full. At three twenty-eight *Columbia* changed spinnakers, hoisting *Vim*'s red top which had been lent to her by Captain Matthews. At three thirty-four both gybed again for the mark and it appeared that *Sceptre* had a good lead.

During this race a strange craft was seen in the arena which was kept sacred to all but a few. It was in close company with the famous Morris Rosenfeld's launch with the white flag FOTO. The stranger wore a green flag: BEKEN, COWES, and was manned by Keith Beken, armed as he was with various cameras including his famous box, held with both hands, with a squeeze bulb held in the mouth operating the shutter. It seemed most courteous of the New York Yacht Club to allow the leading yacht photographers on both sides of the Atlantic to operate side by side. *Sceptre*'s crew may have been heartened by the sight of Beken's banner, but probably wished for some real Cowes weather. *Sceptre* rounded the first mark a minute and five seconds ahead of *Columbia* to noisy applause, and the members of the Syndicate on board *Vergemere* looked very happy. It was a close fetch to the next mark and *Columbia* started to gain fast. About half way down the leg she sailed clean through *Sceptre*'s lee, well to leeward, the distance being given by *Sceptre* as a couple of hundred yards and by *Columbia* as seventy-five. This was at a press conference after the race, at which Colin Ratsey represented the challenger and Olin Stephens the defender. If there is a lesson to be learnt from these meetings, it is the great advantage of having the last word, as one can cap anything said by one's opponent. It is merely one of the finer points of 'Pressmanship'.

About a mile and a half from the mark *Columbia* changed jibs and *Sceptre* set the 'genaker', a small flat sail which looked like a high-cut genoa but was set on the spinnaker pole tacked down. This did not seem to pay her as it backwinded the mainsail quite badly and she rounded 45 seconds astern of *Columbia*. As both boats had to sail at eight knots dead to windward to the finish in the light wind the race was virtually over. *Columbia* tacked to cover *Sceptre* as she rounded the mark and at one time on the boat which followed the challenger seemed to be sailing fast. She was apparently being driven off, making no attempt to outpoint *Columbia*. However both made no attempt at match racing and after *Columbia* had been put well ahead by a windshift time petered out and the race was declared void.

It had been a useful day's practice for *Sceptre*, and Mann and his crew had shown considerable skill in sailing, particularly downwind. The performance of the challenger both to windward and reaching was disappointing and it was not surprising that they asked for a 'lay day' as allowed by the rules.

The spectator fleet was once again kept well under control by the coast-guard. Captain G. L. Rollins of the *Duane* was establishing quite a reputation as a humorist. His classic remark of the day was directed at a sailing boat which was looking as unhappy as *Sceptre* soon after the start or *Columbia* a little later: 'We understand your situation perfectly, but please don't get excited. We'll just take a little piece off your stern.'

SECOND RACE: 24TH SEPTEMBER

The weather looked a bit more promising for the second race on Wednesday 24th September. The wind as we proceeded out of Newport was S.W. about 10 knots, the best that had been seen so far. The course signalled for the first leg of the triangular course was 230° magnetic, which was a great help to the coast-guard. The previous few days the spectator fleet had come more or less down the track to the first mark. In consequence there had been a lot of very turbulent water and air at the start, which had been particularly noticeable the previous day. On this Wednesday there was a chance to get the spectators behind the starting line without interfering with the weather of the two contestants.

The wind speed at the start was still about 10 knots, and the two helmsmen seemed to look far more likely to make a fight of it. Graham Mann got on Briggs Cunningham's tail soon after the five-minute gun. With about two minutes to go they both gybed, with *Sceptre* short of *Columbia.* At one time it looked as if *Sceptre* was sure of the safe leeward berth, but she seemed to be early and had to bear away to let *Columbia* on to her weather. They started thus with *Sceptre* and the defender beam to beam and there they stayed for the next forty minutes, with *Columbia* gradually eating out on *Sceptre*'s weather. A lot of people criticized Graham Mann for not taking *Columbia* on in a short tacking duel, but it seemed possible that with the still light wind he did not wish to risk killing the challenger stone dead against what was obviously a very much faster boat. He pointed out that he had his wind clear and had he tacked he would have had to sail through Columbia's dirty wind.

At about seven minutes past one both boats tacked and *Sceptre* appeared to be very slightly to weather of *Columbia*'s track. She was about five hundred yards behind, but her sails looked far better in the slightly stronger wind than that of the last few days. The wind by now was about 8 to 10 knots and showed signs of lightening as they both approached the mark. *Columbia* tacked to round it at one forty-one, with *Sceptre* three minutes and three seconds astern, having had to pinch round it, when the wind fell very light on her indeed.

Columbia set the red top spinnaker loaned by *Vim*, known to her crew as 'Little Harry' after the Navigator's red head, and *Sceptre* hoisted the red, white, and blue Herbulot, both crews took about thirty seconds for the operation. They continued like this until two fifteen, when *Sceptre* lowered her spinnaker, setting a genoa and luffing apparently to find more wind. This manœuvre was much criticized. The object was to find more wind up to the southward, which had been forecast, and about ten minutes later the genaker was set. This sail proved of very doubtful efficiency and this in turn was lowered and eventually the white and green striped Herbulot was set, at two thirty-five. This was lowered just short of the mark, and she gybed with genoa set. She then luffed to weather of the course to try to pick up more wind again and with the new jib, which had been made during the previous day when Colin Ratsey made an early morning flit to City Island to supervise its cutting, amid much speculation as to his objects. *Columbia* had gybed her spinnaker round the second mark 8 minutes and 55 seconds ahead, which seemed incredible, and kept her Hood sail full until the finish, although it was setting very shy on the later stages. Mann again luffed on the leg home which did not seem to pay although being behind he had to try something different. It was not until *Columbia* had finished that *Sceptre* set a spinnaker and it seemed that she was either determined to go down with colours flying or that she was indicating by this rather large red, white, and blue sail, which was the same colours as Flag C, that she was willing to start on the morrow. That flag was hoisted in the lee rigging.

Times:	*Columbia*	3	17	43
	Sceptre	3	29	25
			11	42 margin.

One wondered why on earth Graham Mann had not persisted with his Herbulot, sailing down on its best course down the leeward of the mark and then lowering it if necessary, rather than luffing as he did. If one luffed out of the mean course to the next mark there was always the very grave danger of falling into the wind-shadow of some of the larger vessels following the race, whereas to bear away was preferable as the spectators went away from you better. This is in no disparagement to the excellent way in which the fleet of spectator craft was handled by the coast-guard. Captain Rollins of the *Duane* was once more in good voice. As he turned the fleet before the weather mark he cried over the loud speaker to the spectators. 'Swing your partners, you can eliminate the "do-si-do".'

It also seemed possible that the Herbulot spinnaker, at least in that weight of wind, was not a particularly efficient sail for the reaches of the *America*'s Cup course, however good it was on a run.

THIRD RACE: 25TH SEPTEMBER

There was optimism in the *Sceptre* camp as she was towed out ahead of *Columbia* for the first time in the series. The wind was blowing 22 knots from the S.W. and it was obvious that it would continue for a day or two. The start was at twelve ten, and *Sceptre* was to weather of *Columbia* which drove clear and leebowed the challenger. She was forced to tack to clear her wind. *Columbia* tacked over her and was seen to be about five lengths clear already with the race having only lasted four minutes. From then until they rounded the weather mark the two boats went through the motions of match-racing tactics with *Sceptre* breaking tacks with *Columbia* whenever she could. There came a time when *Columbia* was so far ahead that she only tacked to 'shepherd' rather than to try to blanket the challenger, as Olin Stephens explained afterwards. This must have been really rather demoralizing for Graham Mann and Colin Ratsey, who shared the helm on this beat. They rounded 2 minutes and 23 seconds astern of the defender. *Sceptre* had broken two jib sheets on this beat, but from a distance of about a mile aboard the *Duane* this was not noticeable.

Columbia hoisted another red-topped spinnaker borrowed from *Vim*, which was known as 'Big Harry' as opposed to 'Little Harry' which they had set the day before. *Sceptre* gybed before setting the red, white, and blue Herbulot, and set off on a diverging course, which did not seem to pay particularly, as she sailed a greater distance. She gybed, giving her supporters a few anxious moments during the operation, but all was well. *Columbia* lowered her spinnaker some three hundred yards from the mark, but did not set a headsail until just before rounding it, sailing bald-headed for the last few minutes. She gained only six seconds on this run, in spite of *Sceptre* sailing a greater distance, but was too far away for the challenger to make much impression on her during the beat. Once again she shepherded *Sceptre* to windward and after a few quick tacks they settled down to a couple of long boards to the weather mark. It is understood that she had trouble with her coffee grinders. The wind seemed to increase and *Sceptre* looked even more unhappy in the steep seas. She acted like a rocking horse bouncing back and forth while *Columbia*, although making an occasional buck, settled down much quicker and seemed far more sea-kindly. She increased her lead to 7 minutes 45 seconds on this second beat, so that all hope of winning the race was lost.

Sceptre's crew seemed game still and set the spinnaker in very quick time, but in spite of their efforts *Columbia* won by 8 minutes and 20 seconds.

Times:	*Columbia*	3	9	07
	Sceptre	3	17	27
			8	20 margin.

This was very disappointing because many people had regarded *Sceptre* as a good hard weather boat. She had had a chance to prove herself in these conditions and failed, and it appeared obvious that the fourth race would be purely a formality. Both boats signalled their willingness to race the next day and there certainly did not seem to be any point in prolonging this honourable form of slaughter any longer than necessary. *Columbia*'s crew spent the night repairing a broken forestay and at one time one of the rumours, which were rife in Newport at the time, implied that she would not be able to race, but she left her mooring on time the next morning.

At the end of the third race there occurred one of the very few accidents among the spectator fleet. Two boats collided and a man was taken aboard a coast-guard cutter with a very badly injured leg. He was rushed to hospital. The spectator fleet had thinned out quite a lot due to the rather dull racing and also because of the roughish weather. It appears that all through the history of these Cup races there has been this falling off in the strength of the spectators as the races have progressed. Yacht racing, particularly rather unequal match racing, is hardly a spectator sport.

FOURTH RACE: 26TH SEPTEMBER

The wind was once more S.W., about 20 knots, or what the New Englanders refer to as a 'smoky sou'-wester', when

Sceptre, apparently anxious to get the whole business finished, led *Columbia* out to the start once more. The visibility was not as good as the previous day, hence the reference to smoke, and the swell was a bit longer.

The start was very much the same as that in the last race of the final American trials. Graham Mann took Briggs Cunningham the wrong side of the Committee boat, with about a minute to go. Cunningham tacked clear and, gybing, passed under the stern of the *Nor'Easter*. Meanwhile Graham Mann passed round her bow, bore away, and rounded up on the line. Unfortunately at the gun there was three feet of his bow over the line, about the distance from the stem to the forestay. Graham bore away very quickly and took thirteen seconds to recross and clear the line while *Columbia* ploughed through her weather. The race was a repetition of the previous day's massacre. *Columbia* seemed at one time not to be going so well, but maybe this was because the wind was only about 18 knots at times.

The two boats beat up to the weather mark, taking about fourteen tacks and once again *Columbia* shepherded rather than covered *Sceptre*. *Sceptre* had to take two extra tacks for the mark, and on the last one, her weather jib sheet caught on the cleat on top of the winch and had to be cut. It was the first time it had happened. She rounded the mark with the jib aback and was 5 minutes 30 seconds astern. *Columbia* had broken out a small blue-topped spinnaker which had belonged to *Weatherly* and seemed to go very fast on the first reach. *Sceptre* eventually set the red, white, and blue Herbulot, and not holding quite such a good wind set off in pursuit. She seemed to be gaining, but as Colin Ratsey described it after the race, the gremlins were at work. The spinnaker guy parted. Then the spinnaker sheet was caught under the mainboom. When the crew tried to clear it the boat gave a lurch and the weight of wind in the spinnaker acting on the sheet and against the boom vang, broke the main boom, which was only held together by the sail track. This was 'fished' with the boom crutch, and although the boom appeared to be bending quite a lot all was more or less well. Mann, Ratsey, and Bishop had discussed giving up or continuing with the race, before these emergency repairs. The spinnaker boom end fitting then broke off, probably as a result of the jolt when the guy parted. The spinnaker had to be handed and the boom was lashed to the main boom in preparation for the gybe, which in actual fact made the operation easier. She rounded 8 minutes 13 seconds astern.

Neither boat set spinnakers on the last leg and *Sceptre* caught up a bit with her crew singing lustily. The spectators crowded round the finish and *Columbia,* the winner of the seventeenth series for the *America*'s Cup crossed the line to be saluted by the winning gun and the pop of a champagne cork opened by one of her crew. The yachts, destroyers, coast-guard cutters, and other craft saluted her with their whistles, sirens, hooters, and flags, while the Naval tug which acted as the mark played her fire hoses in a colourful fountain.

Times:	*Columbia*	3	04	22	
	Sceptre	3	11	27	
			7	05	margin.

The seventeenth challenger had received just about as big a thrashing as had *Endeavour II* from *Ranger* in 1937, but it seemed that the New York Yacht Club in no way blamed this rather sorry performance on *Sceptre*'s crew. As she finished all U.S. Navy and Coastguard vessels present hoisted the following signal: 'Mortals cannot command success; you and your companions have certainly deserved it.' It was from Commodore Burr Bartram, who quoted the signal from the Nicholas letters made by Lord St. Vincent in answer to Nelson's letter apologizing for his failure to take Tenerife, in 1797. Nelson lost his arm and offered to resign his command, feeling he was no further use.

When the two boats had returned to harbour after cheering each other, as they did after each race, the crews visited each other to compare notes and opinions on equipment. Meanwhile, ashore at the Ida Lewis Yacht Club there was a rather bigger press conference than usual after the day's race to clarify any incidents which were not seen clearly. This time Hugh Goodson was there to make a statement on behalf of the owners. He said, 'The *Sceptre* owners are bitterly disappointed, but we lost to a better boat. . . . The owners have absolutely no criticism of the handling of the boat by the crew and Commander Mann.'

He pointed out that the owners and crew of *Sceptre* were pleased that the series had ended on a happy note for all, indicating that this post-race good feeling had not always been the case. He said that the future of *Sceptre* would be decided definitely on 28th September and in fact, she was to be shipped back to England. He asked for 'five minutes' to think over the question as to whether his Syndicate would build another boat to challenge for the *America*'s Cup. When asked if he thought that, after the solid beating *Sceptre* took, the Royal Yacht Squadron and England in general would abandon future competition for the Cup, he replied, 'Quite frankly I don't think we shall ever give up.'

Then the poor designer was put through the mill. David Boyd looked rather embarrassed but faced the not entirely unsympathetic men present with great courage. He told them that *Sceptre* was based upon two models which were tested in towing tanks. It was not based on any existing Twelve Metre boat, and he said that he had never before designed a boat in the Twelve Metre class. In answer to a question asking what would be the first thing he would do if he were starting to build another Twelve Metre, he replied, 'I would ask Olin Stephens to show me the lines of *Columbia*.' He said that the sea conditions were representative of what they had expected and that conditions had been ideal for *Sceptre*. Asked if the *America*'s Cup might be held in smaller boats, he replied, 'It should be in the biggest boats people can afford to build and race.'

Colin Ratsey then described the incidents during the race and he was followed by John S. Dickerson, Chairman of the Race Committee of the New York Yacht Club, who referred to their long summer, their luck with weather and the excellent sportsmanship in the trials as well as the races.

Henry Sears, Syndicate manager, said that *Columbia* was to be laid up and that her future activities depended upon whether there was Twelve Metre racing in the following season. He also expressed the hope that the *America*'s Cup competition would continue, but said that there might be some changes in the rules for two-boat racing. He said that he thought the Twelve Metres were about as small as the boats ought to be.

Briggs Cunningham remarked that from his viewpoint it had been fun sailing with amateurs. They had had a tougher time beating *Vim* than *Sceptre*, but if it had not been for *Vim* they would not have done so well against *Sceptre*. When asked which of the many sports in which he participated and excelled most suited him he replied, 'At the time I am doing boats, it seems to be the ultimate.' He also confirmed the rumour that *Columbia* carried a book on sailing written by *Weatherly*'s skipper, Arthur Knapp. He said that his crew took a look at *Race Your Boat Right* and did a little better on the starts since they did.

Columbia had carried an ordinary radio aboard and was listening to the broadcast account of the race in an effort perhaps to learn about winds. They had missed the broadcast from the blimp which had been most helpful to them. Pierre Dupont from *Weatherly*'s crew had been broadcasting from the blimp for Columbia Broadcasting System, but that day it had engine trouble. Many people in the spectator fleet had heard Peter Scott from the *Duane* and had become fans of his, not only for his remarks on the racing but also on the wildfowl which he saw during the races. When not actually 'on the air' he had been giving an account to Philip Hays ashore in Newport.

When asked if he favoured a change in the rule for Cup boats, Cunningham replied, 'Design-wise and material-wise we are too restricted by the Twelve Metre rule. I would rather see it sailed in boats capable of ocean sailing like the original schooner *America*, which sailed across the Atlantic and then won her race. Aluminium and fibreglass are among the materials for hull construction which might be utilized, and more people would build boats for the race if we do this.' Asked if he would sail a Twelve Metre across the Atlantic he replied, 'Sailing a Twelve across the Atlantic is like those fellows paddling canoes across—not much point in it.' He said that if the rule could be changed it would work for greater improvement of boat design.

Last of all there was Olin Stephens, who expressed the view that it was possible that the broader sections of *Sceptre*'s hull forward could have something to do with making her slower than *Columbia*.

On the Saturday night the crews dined together at Beechbound, the large mansion rented for the season by the *Columbia* syndicate. The crew of *Sceptre* presented each of *Columbia*'s crew with a wooden shield with the R.Y.S. burgee and in return received a china plate with *Columbia* upon it. After that proceedings became less formal and Rod Stephens sang. The party lasted until the small hours and continued at Horsehead until the morning, bagpipes and all. On the Sunday Mayor Henry Wilkinson, of Newport, presented both skippers with silver trays, and other members with tiles with the Newport crest. Later on that Sunday afternoon at Horsehead, Jamestown, Mr. and Mrs. Sydney Wright were presented with Armada plate ash trays and *Sceptre*'s racing flag by Hugh Goodson. Mrs. Margaret Harris received a silver salver, the cook a brooch, and the maids chain bracelets. It was all over, and as the crew began to disperse homeward bound it was like the end of term at school.

CONCLUSION

So history has repeated itself for the seventeenth time and as the final pages of this book have been written there has been much discussion as to the future of the contests for the Cup. Those who read Part One may have noted a similarity between the efforts of the *Sceptre* Syndicate and those of the owners of *Thistle*, in 1887. Both yachts were designed by newcomers to the Cup competition and both were built on the Clyde under a veil of secrecy. The owners of both were optimistic and their boats were soundly thrashed. In the New York Yacht Club model room there are models of each defender and challenger side by side. With a very few exceptions the design of the defender seems to have been a step ahead of the challenger.

There was *Shamrock V*, which could probably have been beaten by any of the three boats built in America at the time as possible defenders. I have no doubt that *Weatherly*, *Easterner*, and *Vim* could have defended successfully against *Sceptre*. *Sceptre* appears to have been beaten in the design stage, maybe in the tank as *Endeavour II* was by *Ranger*. Probably, above all there was the genius of Olin and Rod Stephens. It seems a pity that so few British designers have a follow-up organization comparable to that of these two famous brothers. They not only design a boat to the very last detail, but they also make absolutely certain that she is sailed and tuned to perfection. At a press interview before the races Olin Stephens was asked whether he had any lucky charms or suchlike aboard *Columbia*. He replied, 'I have a superstition about not being superstitious.' In other words, he leaves nothing to chance.

Many suggested after the races that the crews should have changed boats and raced against each other. This suggestion could only have come from those who never saw the races. I have absolutely no doubt that *Columbia* would have proved better. In actual fact the crew of *Sceptre* dispersed very soon after the races finished. This was perhaps a pity, because a race had been organized at Seawanhaka Corinthian Y.C. for the Twelve Metres the following week-end, and Hugh Goodson had been offered the helm of *Columbia*. He left in the *Queen Mary* on 1st October and so could not accept.

There seems to be no doubt that *Sceptre* was beaten by a better boat in all conditions. It appeared that the only point of sailing in which she really could hold her own, if not beat *Columbia*, was a run with one of Herbulot's superb spinnakers set. As far as hull form is concerned the story may well be told by the photographs of each boat. *Sceptre* was also narrower aft than *Columbia*. The dimensions of each as published in Lloyd's register are as follows:

	Sceptre	*Columbia*
L.O.A.	68′ 8″	69′ 7″
L.W.L.	46′ 6″	45′ 10″
Beam	11′ 9″	11′ 8″
Draught	9′ 1″	8′ 11″

The sail area of *Sceptre* can be judged from the sail plan and the schedule of sails. The displacement was given in several publications as 68,000 lbs, but that of the boat whose model was known to Saunders-Roe as Boyd 'B' was 63,000. This is considerably more than the 56,800 lbs said to be the displacement of *Columbia*, although this may not be correct.

It is said that a model of *Sceptre* will be tested, together with that of *Flica II* at the Stephens Institute, Hoboken, New Jersey. A very kind invitation to members of the *Sceptre* party to visit this test tank was extended to them just after the races. David Boyd's 'B' model was broken soon after the tank tests, so no doubt a new model will have to be made for these tests, which may well prove interesting to Mr. Crago, whose tank came under some criticism immediately after the races. I am told that results obtained from tank tests can vary from time to time owing to various factors such as water temperature, air temperature, distortion of models and the human errors involved. When Olin Stephens submits a design for tank testing he tests it with all previous designs which he has produced of the same class, so that his experience in this field is probably far greater than any other yacht designer.

In fairness to Mr. Crago, Frank Murdoch, and Colonel Perry, regarding the tank tests carried out by Saunders-Roe on the models submitted by the four designers during the summer of 1957, it should be pointed out that the tank was only to be used as a referee to choose the designer. Mr. Crago in particular regretted that the tank was not used as an aid to the development of the best possible model. Even if David Boyd had wanted to try to improve on his models, there was too little time to test in the tank any improvement which he might have made. Frank Murdoch was not himself concerned with the actual form of the boats, but only in producing an order of merit from the figures obtained from the tank tests. Incidentally the critical wind speeds were considered to be from eight to twelve knots, which makes it slightly mystifying that *Sceptre* should always have been labelled a heavy-weather boat. That the tank test results as obtained by Saunders-Roe were all close suggests that they were a pretty reasonable comparison of the models submitted. That *Sceptre* was so badly beaten seems to explode the theory that the Twelve Metre class is virtually a one-design. Anyone who saw *Sceptre*, *Columbia*, *Weatherly*, and *Vim* out of the water at Newport will have rejected it in any case.

As this book has had to be written as a more or less 'blow by blow' account of the life of the seventeenth challenger, impressions of some periods of her life may well have been clouded by enthusiasm. The pity of it all was that the mere beating of *Evaine*, which she seemed to accomplish in the later stages about as easily as *Columbia* beat her, was not enough. Owen Aisher's trial horse, which was so valuable early in the season was never really good enough to extend the challenger enough during July 1958, nor was she good enough to establish her definitely as unlikely to beat a faster boat than *Vim*. It is only in really top class competition that the little details, which H. S. Vanderbilt described as 'the little drops of water and little grains of sand', can be attended to with any certainty as to whether they make any difference, or not.

David Boyd has designed several very good Six Metres, without a failure, and there are those who suggest that as they have all proved somewhat difficult to tune up, *Sceptre* may not have reached the high state of tuning which was apparently reached by *Columbia*. For instance when she sailed in England she had her mast nearly dead upright, when in Newport she had it slightly raked. There were some who suggested that one was correct, and some even vehemently suggested that it was not raked enough. Would it have paid to move the whole sail plan, mast and all, further aft or further forward? Maybe time will produce the answer, which can only be found if she ever sails in close competition.

Her mast seemed to stand up as well as *Columbia*'s, although some of the fittings on it, such as the 'sky hook' for locking the head of the mainsail aloft looked rather more cumbersome than those in the defender. The latter, in common with all the American Twelves had a luff rope groove, which seemed more tidy than *Sceptre*'s track and slides. The question of the right tension of the rigging can also only be decided by experience in strong competition. Some boats like their rigging slack, some tight. This is not meant in any way to disparage the efforts of those responsible for trying to tune *Sceptre* up, but only to point out the lack of assistance from really strong competition.

I have already mentioned sails. There seems to be little doubt that we can produce material comparable to the best American synthetic cloth. The pounding action of the boat probably made some of *Sceptre*'s sails look poorer than they were, but our sailmakers almost certainly lack experience of cutting synthetic sails of the size required by a Twelve Metre, whereas *Vim* started the season with sails from three different lofts and finished with a lot more. The defender was lent some of the best of *Weatherly* and *Vim*'s sails, having already collected a total of some thirty-three of her own. That it was necessary to remedy a deficiency of good full-sized light weather sails in *Sceptre*'s locker, when one race had already been lost in such conditions and another saved by the time limit seemed remarkable, as did the fact that the headsail made by Watts, although a good one, seemed to be much smaller than necessary.

Sceptre's Herbulot spinnakers were superior to any of those set by the defender on the runs and her crew earned much praise for the way in which they handled them. The technique of setting a Herbulot and of keeping it drawing with maximum efficiency is different from any other spinnakers. It was therefore quite amusing to listen to the comments of some American spinnaker hands when they first saw these sails set by *Sceptre*. They had been reared on various textbooks which laid down fairly rigid rules which are often broken when setting a Herbulot. It was interesting to see that the American foredeck hands did not appear to mind dropping their jibs into the water when setting spinnakers, indeed some felt that the very slight momentary loss in speed might have helped the spinnaker to get drawing better. *Sceptre* might perhaps have fared better when reaching on the triangular course with a smaller sail than the Herbulot, but as she was astern she simply had to try what seemed to be her only 'ace'.

Some of *Sceptre*'s fittings looked rustic compared with the beautiful ones in most of the American Twelves. There may well be something to be said for abolishing the blacksmith's shop in our yacht yards and really taking fittings a bit more seriously. So many British yachts are beautifully built, but their appearance is ruined by heavy galvanized ironmongery.

The genoa winches made by Leyland Motors seemed to work extremely well. The rather heavy veering gear had been removed. Each of these winches was man enough to sheet the jib in as quickly as the Americans, who had to use both their winches in tandem to do so. In fact one of their criticisms was that with the large cockpit *Sceptre*'s crew would not be able to use their winches in tandem. They did not have to.

Graham Mann said he liked *Columbia*'s compass arrangement and also the reels for stowing sheet and runner tails. *Columbia* had a quite ingenious device for bringing the lee shroud inboard a few inches, to keep it clear of the genoa.

The large cockpit seemed to be a help to the crew and gave no trouble on the rougher days. Some Americans questioned whether it was aerodynamically sound. It seems possible that such a thing will be banned in future Twelve Metres, because Hugh Goodson and David Boyd cabled the Royal Yachting Association from New York suggesting that a motion to revise the rules concerning cabin fittings and deck openings should be considered at the 1958 International Yacht Racing Union Conference. Unfortunately the agenda for this meeting had already been closed.

That the crew rose to the occasion magnificently will come as no surprise to those who have watched recent Olympic games. We are sometimes a bit late in getting organized, but our crews seldom give anything away when really in the thick of it. The Americans are always fortunate in having an almost unlimited supply of young men of really tremendous sailing experience for their years. As I have already mentioned, I consider that the crew selection trials were a bit overdone. It was good to give as many people as possible a trial, but I believe that it did interfere with essential tuning. *Sceptre* was launched on 2nd April, and those who were to be her Cup race crew were not in her together as a body until 23rd June, which seems to have been much too long. There are so many imponderables connected with a new racing yacht that it is well to reduce the most important of all, the human element, to the simplest possible form as soon as possible. It is interesting to note that those in charge of the defender had some difficulty in attuning their crew, which was composed largely of experienced offshore sailors, to the higher tempo of match racing.

The *Sceptre* Syndicate embarked upon a very bold venture, which to my mind deserved better success. At times the organization tended to appear to creak, mainly because there seemed to be a danger of there being 'too many cooks'. I am assured, and indeed am quite certain, that at all times the members of the Syndicate were on friendly terms with each other. That they were not served by some as well as they had hoped was a very great pity. The tendency to over-emphasize secrecy was also a pity. In any case in such a venture it is almost impossible to maintain it. As an example, I was told the dimensions of *Sceptre*'s biggest spinnaker within twelve hours of arriving in Newport, five weeks before the races started. We had little difficulty in finding out how *Vim* gybed her spinnaker. Management of a syndicate boat is always a problem, but there is no reason why those who pay the piper should not call the tune. The Mercer syndicate, who owned *Weatherly*, was content to leave the running of the boat to the designer and the skipper. On the other hand the *Columbia* syndicate had two members, Briggs Cunningham and Henry Sears, on board the boat, as were the designer, Olin, and his brother Rod Stephens. Boats and crews tend not to respond to committees or democracy; they require dictatorial command. It requires considerable skill to find the right dictator.

At this early stage it is not known where the next challenge will come from. There were rumours flying about that challenges were expected from Australia, Canada, the Argentine, Cuba and Sweden. Whoever does challenge is almost certainly wasting his money unless there is really strong opposition against which to tune up at home. The Americans have almost always been fortunate in having enough really good boats to make a fight for the honour of defending the Cup, while we have so often challenged with a boat which has never floated and which has had little prospect of the really hard racing which the defender has had. Only in the case of the *Endeavours*, which had *Velsheda* against which to tune up, has the challenger ever had close competition.

The question immediately arises, where does this competition come from? There has only been one International Twelve Metre built in Europe since the war, and that is *Sceptre*. The fate of the boats of the pre-war British Twelve Metre fleet has already been mentioned. If the future Cup races are to be held in Twelve Metres, then there appears to be only one answer and that is to try to collect the best boats in Europe and America for at least one season's racing in British waters. This might possibly encourage new owners into the class as the prospect of close racing would perhaps overcome the objections to building such a boat on the grounds of cost. It should also be made quite clear by any challenging club that they are prepared to enter the best boat available, provided it complies with the regulations as to designing and building, and regardless of whether the owner was a member of that club or not. According to the Deed of Gift the challenging yacht must be constructed in the country from which the challenge is made. The Livingstone brothers from Sydney obtained a ruling from the New York Yacht Club that 'constructed' means 'designed and built'. The question of membership of most clubs is really only a formality, and it is worthy of note that there was not a single member of the Royal Yacht Squadron in *Sceptre*'s racing crew. The R.Y.S. was given the power to substitute another yacht up to a week before the races by the seventeenth Cup race conditions.

The question really arises whether the present Twelve Metre is a suitable boat with which to persevere. As already mentioned some feel that it is not, while others love them dearly. There is a strong feeling in the New York Yacht Club that to hold the Cup races in an offshore racing type of boat would be akin to running the Derby with cart horses. The question of having a longer course has already been mentioned and here the New York Yacht Club consider that there are enough major offshore racing events.

Neither the Cruising Club of America nor the Royal Ocean Racing Club rules in themselves are suitable as those to which to build Cup racers. It is possible that the new cruiser/racer rule may be, particularly now that steps are being taken to provide a class to it which will fit inside the 44-foot water-line length limit laid down by the amended Deed of Gift. So many would prefer to see, and some might even be persuaded to buy, a boat which had a sea-kindly enough hull form for it to be able to enter offshore events, when its Cup race days were done, with a hope of giving the owner a chance of winning and not too much discomfort. It is always possible that whatever class future contests are raced in, they may be virtually killed by the genius of Olin Stephens.

I am told by Sandy Haworth that in 1931, when the late Malden Heckstall-Smith was going down to Plymouth to work out the times for the Fastnet race of that year, he stopped at a teashop and when he had finished he was asked to sign the visitors' book. Olin Stephens had designed a small day boat, and *Dorade*, with which he had been second in the 1930 Bermuda Race, first in the 1931 Transatlantic and was even in the Fastnet race, was his first big boat. Instead of writing the eulogistic comment in the book, which the proprietor obviously expected, that old sage wrote, 'I am going to meet the finest yacht designer in the world.' What a prophetic statement, made when Olin Stephens was only twenty-three.

There is a suggestion that it is only necessary to make a few more regulations about cabin fittings for Twelve Metres in order to encourage new owners. While this may be true, it should be remembered that when the Twelves were in their heyday, before the war, they were raced by eight men. The most practical way of accommodating the present crews of eleven seems to be a battery of pipe cots, with a galley and bathroom. Rules as to accommodation with all their ramifications are invariably reduced to a farce, and one day the makers of yacht racing rules will discover that the only practical way of enforcing accommodation rules is to make the crew live aboard. These are entirely my own views on the subject. No doubt better men than I will thrash them out and produce answers with which many will not agree, but that is one of the great joys of the sport.

About a week after the Cup races I was sitting in the bar of the New York Yacht Club with Graham Mann. He looked at the gap in the curtain to the Trophy Room, turned and with a laugh said, 'That ruddy cup is still there.' He thought for a moment and continued, 'I can see now why it gets 'em.'

Only if one has been involved at all with the hurry, the fuss, the rumours, the muddles, and all that goes to give the races for it the biggest build-up of any sporting event, can anyone really appreciate what this Cup means. I am told on good authority that the 1937 Cup races received five times more space in the American newspapers than did the whole of the 1936 Olympic Games.

Many of those who brought their boats to join the vast spectator fleet were longing for us to win. This was not out of any disloyalty, but was simply because they wanted a really good excuse to bring their boats across to Britain. What an incredible invasion it would have meant. It certainly might have done our yachting industry the most enormous amount of good, and should certainly be borne in mind by those who tend rather pompously to condemn our participation in the Cup races at all.

It seemed a pity when the races were over that they had been held so late in the season. *Vim* had gone back to Oyster Bay, while *Weatherly* and *Easterner* lay forlornly at their moorings. What a fine thing it would be if future challenges could be earlier in the year, so that challenger and defender could join in the New York Yacht Club cruise, with the other

American yachts, battling together and joining the same parties with the cares of the Cup races behind them. The *Endeavours* did so in 1937, and it seems to be a process which should be repeated.

I am sure that there will be future challenges for this elusive and glamorous trophy. Already some members of the *Sceptre* Syndicate have expressed their intention of trying again. Perhaps their best chance would be to make it a combined Commonwealth challenge, with final trials at Halifax, or even off Newport.

The twelve gentlemen of the *Sceptre* Syndicate bore their defeat with the air of the true sportsmen which they are. That I, as well as others, should have criticized their actions at times has been inevitable, but invariably it has been only in the desire to see their vessel fare better. The story of a failure is never much fun to write, and one can only hope that the lessons which were learnt off Newport and beforehand will be noted by those who come after. Hugh Goodson and his friends have certainly bought experience dearly. The fine crew which they took to America made many good friends among the skilful and delightful men whom they met ashore and afloat, which is the really pleasing aspect of the whole challenge.

When they went to Buckingham Palace before the races, to be received by the Duke of Edinburgh, he referred to them jokingly as 'the mugs'. There is yet another 'mug', that which Sir Thomas Lipton referred to as 'The Ould Mug', which reposes in the New York Yacht Club. As long as it does so it will probably be regarded as the British Yachtsman's Mount Everest.

List of Crews

SCEPTRE	*COLUMBIA*
Captain Stanley Bishop	Briggs Cunningham
Graham Mann	Captain Fred Lawton
Joe Brooks	Olin Stephens
David Boyd Jr.	Henry Sears
C. Colin Ratsey	Halsey Herreshoff
Hamish Connell	Colin Ratsey
Ian Lennox	Rod Stephens
Tim Langford	C. 'Glit' Shields Jr.
Denis Jackson	Victor Romagna
Mike Tremlett	Jimmy Halsam
Charles de Selincourt	Wally Tobin

APPENDIXES

APPENDIX A

RESULTS OF PREVIOUS *AMERICAS*'S CUP RACES

Date		Yacht	Course	Time Allowance m. s.	Elapsed Time h.	m.	s.	Corrected Time h.	m.	s.	Wins by m.	s.
22nd August	1851	*America*	Round Isle of Wight	—	10	37	00	10	37	00	21	00
		Aurora		—	10	58	00	10	58	00		
8th August	1870	*Magic*	N.Y.Y.C. course	—	4	07	54	3	58	26	39	12
		Cambria (10th)		—	4	34	57	4	37	38		
16th October	1871	*Columbia*	N.Y.Y.C. course	—	6	17	42	6	19	41	27	04
		Livonia		—	6	43	00	6	46	45		
18th October	1871	*Columbia*	20 miles to windward	—	3	01	33½	3	07	41¾	10	33¾
		Livonia	off Sandy Hook L.V. and return	—	3	06	49½	3	18	15½		
19th October	1871	*Livonia*	N.Y.Y.C. course	—	3	53	05	4	02	25	15	10
		Columbia[1]		—	4	12	38	4	17	35		
21st October	1871	*Sappho*	20 miles to windward	—	5	33	24	5	36	02	33	21
		Livonia	off Sandy Hook L.V. and return	—	6	04	38	6	09	23		
25th October	1871	*Sappho*	N.Y.Y.C. course	—	4	38	05	4	46	17	25	27
		Livonia		—	5	04	41	5	11	44		

[1] Disabled

APPENDIX A

Date		Yacht	Course	Time Allowance m.	s.	Elapsed Time h.	m.	s.	Corrected Time h.	m.	s.	Wins by m.	s.
11th August	1876	*Madelaine*	N.Y.Y.C. course	0	59	5	24	55	5	23	54	10	59
		Countess of Dufferin				5	34	53	5	34	53		
12th August	1876	*Madelaine*	20 miles to windward off Sandy Hook L.V. and return	0	59	7	19	47	7	18	46	27	14
		Countess of Dufferin				7	46	00	7	46	00		
9th November	1881	*Mischief*	N.Y.Y.C. course			4	17	09	4	17	09	28	$20\frac{1}{4}$
		Atalanta		3	05	4	28	$24\frac{1}{2}$	4	45	$29\frac{1}{4}$		
10th November	1881	*Mischief*	16 miles to leeward off Sandy Hook and return			4	54	53	4	54	53	38	54
		Atalanta		3	05	5	36	52	5	33	47		
14th September	1885	*Puritan*	N.Y.Y.C. course			6	06	05	6	06	05	16	19
		Genesta		0	28	6	22	52	6	22	24		
16th September	1885	*Puritan*	20 miles to leeward off Sandy Hook L.V. and return			5	03	14	5	03	14	1	38
		Genesta		0	28	5	05	20	5	04	52		
9th September	1886	*Mayflower*	N.Y.Y.C. course			5	26	41	5	26	41	12	02
		Galatea		0	38	5	39	21	5	38	43		
11th September	1886	*Mayflower*	20 miles to leeward off Sandy Hook L.V and return			6	49	00	6	49	00	29	09
		Galatea		0	39	7	18	48	7	18	09		

27th September	1887	*Volunteer*	N.Y.Y.C. course			4	53	18	4	53	18	19	$23\frac{3}{4}$
		Thistle		0	05	5	12	$46\frac{3}{4}$	5	12	$41\frac{3}{4}$		
30th September	1887	*Volunteer*	20 miles to windward			5	42	$56\frac{1}{4}$	5	42	$56\frac{1}{4}$	11	$48\frac{3}{4}$
		Thistle	off Scotland L.V. and return	0	06	5	54	51	5	54	45		
7th October	1893	*Vigilant*	15 miles to windward			4	05	47	4	05	47	5	48
		Valkyrie II	off Scotland L.V. and return	1	48	4	13	23	4	11	35		
9th October	1893	*Vigilant*	Triangular course:			3	25	01	3	25	01	10	35
		Valkyrie II	10 miles to each leg	1	48	3	37	24	3	35	36		
13th October	1893	*Vigilant*	15 miles to windward			3	24	39	3	24	39	0	40
		Valkyrie II[1]	off Scotland L.V. and return	1	33	3	26	52	3	25	19		
7th September	1895	*Defender*	15 miles to windward	0	29	5	00	24	4	59	55	8	49
		Valkyrie III	off Scotland L.V. and return			5	08	44	5	08	44		
10th September	1895	*Defender*	Triangular course:	0	29	3	56	25	3	55	56		
		Valkyrie III[2]	10 miles to each leg			3	55	09	3	55	09		
12th September	1895	*Defender*	15 miles to windward	0	29	4	44	12	4	43	43		
		Valkyrie III[3]	off Sandy Hook L.V. and return				—			—			
16th October	1899	*Columbia*	15 miles E.S.E. from			4	53	53	4	53	53	10	08
		Shamrock I	Sandy Hook L.V. and return	0	06	5	04	07	5	04	01		

[1] Remeasured. [2] Disqualified for fouling *Defender*. [3] Withdrew on crossing the line.

APPENDIX A

Date		Yacht	Course	Time Allowance m.	s.	Elapsed Time h.	m.	s.	Corrected Time h.	m.	s.	Wins by m.	s.
17th October	1899	*Columbia*	Triangular course:			3	37	00	3	37	00		
		Shamrock I[1]	10 miles to each leg	0	06		—			—			
20th October	1899	*Columbia*	15 miles S. by W.	0	43	3	38	52	3	38	09	6	34
		Shamrock I	from Sandy Hook L.V. and return			3	44	43	3	44	43		
28th September	1901	*Columbia*	15 miles E. by S. from	0	43	4	31	07	4	30	24	1	20
		Shamrock II	Sandy Hook L.V. and return			4	31	44	4	31	44		
3rd October	1901	*Columbia*	Triangular course:	0	43	3	13	18	3	12	35	3	35
		Shamrock II	10 miles to each leg			3	16	10	3	16	10		
4th October	1901	*Columbia*	15 miles S.S.E. from	0	43	4	33	40	4	32	57	0	41
		Shamrock II	Sandy Hook L.V. and return			4	33	38	4	33	38		
22nd August	1903	*Reliance*	15 miles to windward			3	32	17	3	32	17	7	02
		Shamrock III	off Sandy Hook L.V. and return	1	57	3	41	17	3	39	20		
25th August	1903	*Reliance*	Triangular course:			3	14	54	3	14	54	1	19
		Shamrock III	10 miles to each leg	1	57	3	18	10	3	16	13		
3rd September	1903	*Reliance*	15 miles to windward			4	28	00	4	28	00		
		Shamrock III	off Sandy Hook L.V. and return	1	57	— Did Not Finish —							

15th July	1920	*Shamrock IV*	15 miles to windward			4	20	37	4	20	37			
		Resolute[2]	off Sandy Hook L.V.	7	01		—			—				
			and return											
20th July	1920	*Shamrock IV*	Triangular course:			5	22	18	5	22	18		2	26
		Resolute	10 miles to each leg	7	01	5	31	45	5	24	44			
21st July	1920	*Resolute*	15 miles to windward	7	01	4	03	06	3	56	05		7	01
		Shamrock IV	off Sandy Hook L.V.			4	03	06	4	03	06			
			and return											
23rd July	1920	*Resolute*	Triangular course:	6	40	3	37	52	3	31	12		9	58
		Shamrock IV[3]	10 miles to each leg			3	41	10	3	41	10			
27th July	1920	*Resolute*	15 miles to windward	6	40	5	33	15	5	28	33		19	45
		Shamrock IV	off Sandy Hook L.V.	—		5	48	20	5	48	20			
			and return											
13th September	1930	*Enterprise*	15 miles to leeward	—		4	03	48		—			2	52
		Shamrock V	off Sandy Hook L.V.	—		4	06	40		—				
			and return											
15th September	1930	*Enterprise*	Triangular course:	—		4	00	44		—			9	34
		Shamrock V	10 miles to each leg	—		4	10	18		—				
17th September	1930	*Enterprise*	15 miles to windward	—		3	54	16		—				
		Shamrock V[4]	off Sandy Hook L.V.	—			—			—				
			and return											
18th September	1930	*Enterprise*	Triangular course:	—		3	10	13		—			5	44
		Shamrock V	10 miles to each leg	—		3	15	57		—				

[1] Carried away topmast and withdrew. [2] Throat halyard rendered on winch drum and withdrew. [3] Remeasured.
[4] Main halyard parted and withdrew.

APPENDIX A

Date		Yacht	Course	Time Allowance m. s.	Elapsed Time h.	m.	s.	Corrected Time h. m. s.	Wins by m.	s.
17th September	1934	*Endeavour*	15 miles to windward	—	3	38	44	—	2	09
		Rainbow	off Brenton Reef	—	3	40	53	—		
			L.V. and return							
18th September	1934	*Endeavour*	Triangular course:	—	3	09	01	—	0	50
		Rainbow	10 miles to each leg	—	3	09	51	—		
20th September	1934	*Rainbow*	15 miles to leeward	—	4	15	00	—	3	25
		Endeavour	off Brenton Reef	—	4	18	25	—		
			L.V. and return							
21st September	1934	*Rainbow*	Triangular course:	—	3	55	38	—	1	15
		Endeavour	10 miles to each leg	—	3	56	53	—		
24th September	1934	*Rainbow*	15 miles to leeward	—	3	34	05	—	4	01
		Endeavour	off Brenton Reef	—	3	38	06	—		
			L.V. and return							
26th September	1934	*Rainbow*	Triangular course:	—	3	20	05	—	0	55
		Endeavour	10 miles to each leg	—	3	21	00	—		
31st July	1937	*Ranger*	15 miles to windward	—	4	41	15	—	17	05
		Endeavour II	off Brenton Reef	—	4	58	20	—		
			L.V. and return							
2nd August	1937	*Ranger*	Triangular course:	—	3	41	33	—	18	32
		Endeavour II	10 miles to each leg	—	4	00	05	—		

4th August	1937	*Ranger*	15 miles to windward	—	3	54	30	—	4	27
		Endeavour II	off Brenton Reef	—	3	58	57	—		
			L.V. and return							
5th August	1937	*Ranger*	Triangular course:	—	3	07	49	—	3	37
		Endeavour II	10 miles to each leg	—	3	11	26	—		

APPENDIX B

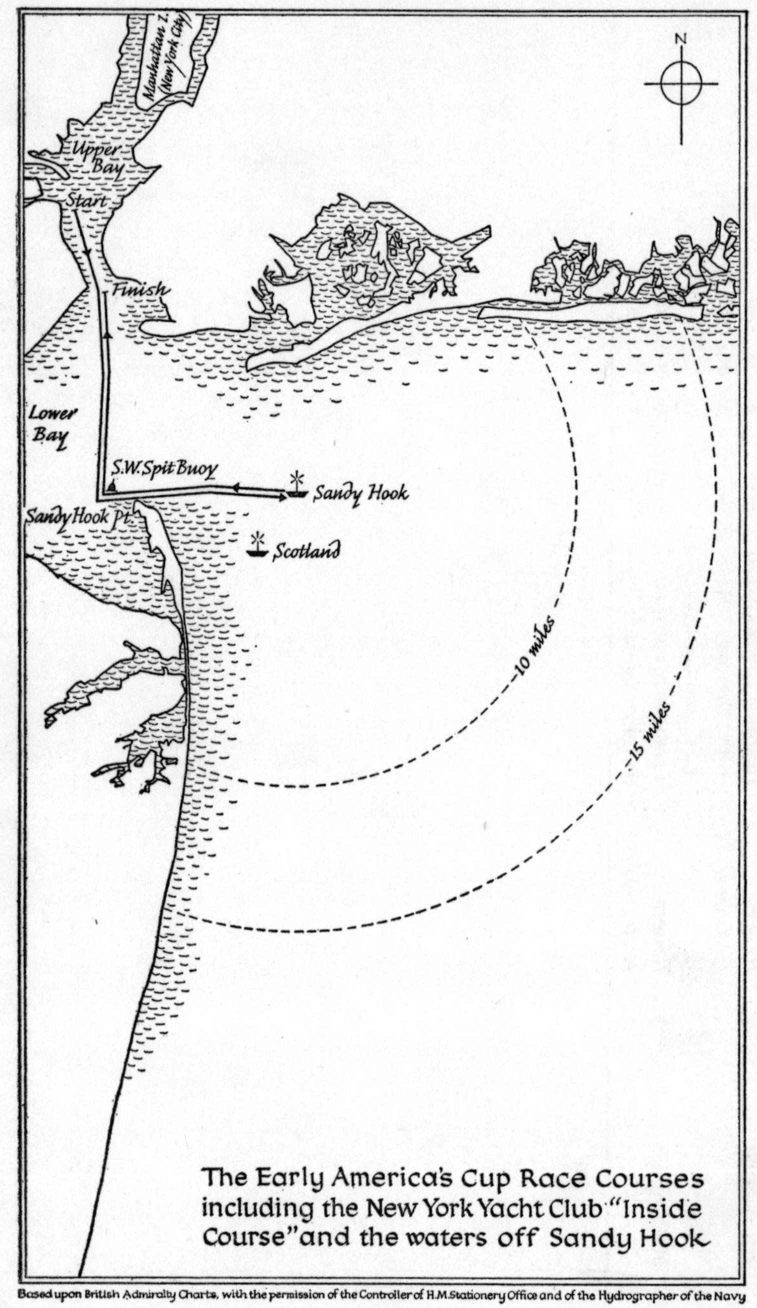

Based upon British Admiralty Charts, with the permission of the Controller of H.M. Stationery Office and of the Hydrographer of the Navy

APPENDIX B

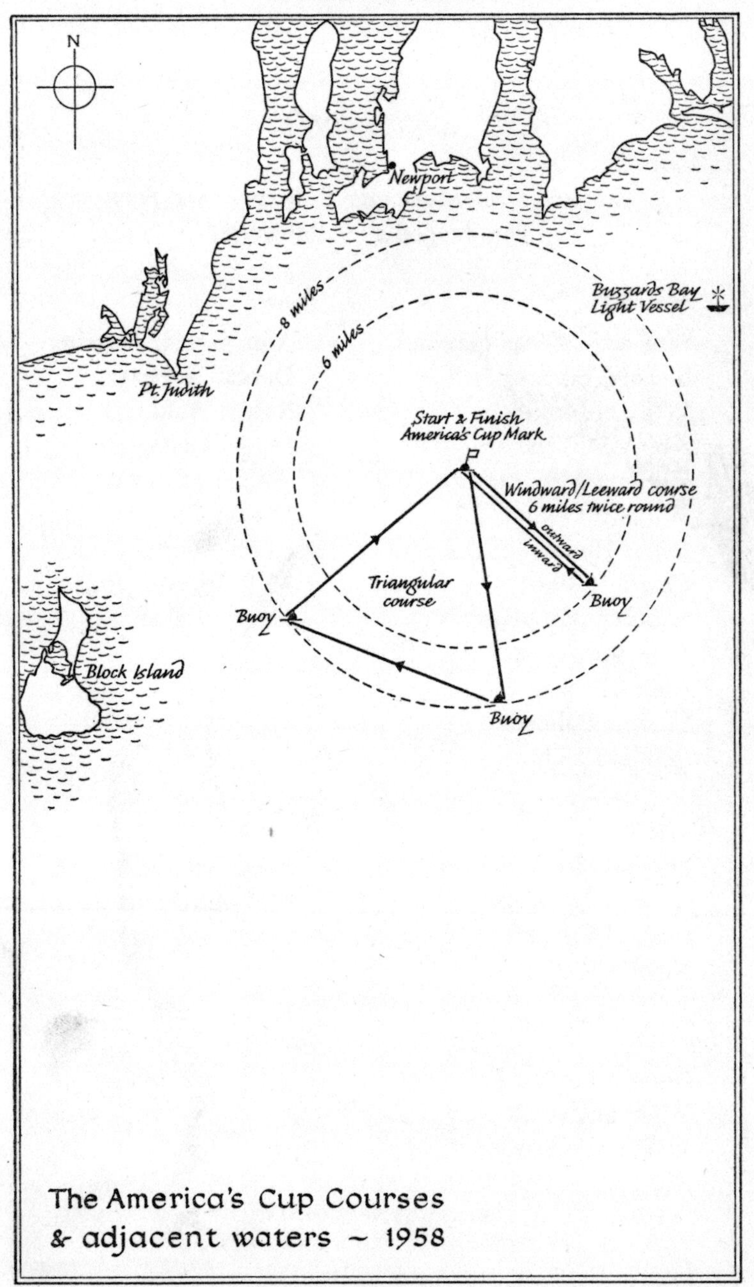

Based upon British Admiralty Charts, with the permission of the Controller of H.M. Stationery Office and of the Hydrographer of the Navy

APPENDIX C

Employees of Alexander Robertson and Sons
who helped to build *Sceptre*

Carpenters

Sam Auld, *Head Foreman*
Richard Murray
William Cameron
Niven McVicar
William McVicar
William Ponton
James Hunter
Charles Sillars
Robert Colquhoun
Alex McQueen
Alex Ritchie
Charles Polmeer
William Yule

Joiners

Alex Grant, *Foreman*
Duncan Barclay
Robert Auld
Daniel Gallagher
William Probert
Walter Polmeer
Hugh Hunter
Malcolm McLachlan
James Graham

Blacksmiths

Duncan Hope, *Foreman*
Andrew Robinson
John McLean
Neville McKenzie

Riggers

Alan Campbell
Malcolm McLachlan

Painters

George Leitch, *Foreman*
William Carroll
William Johnstone

Sawyer

APPENDIX D

RATING FORMULA

$$\frac{L+2D+\sqrt{SA}-F}{2\cdot37} = 12 \text{ Metres}$$

L = Corrected length at 7″ above L.W.L.

D = Skin girth minus chain girth

SA = Mainsail plus 85% Fore triangle

F = Freeboard

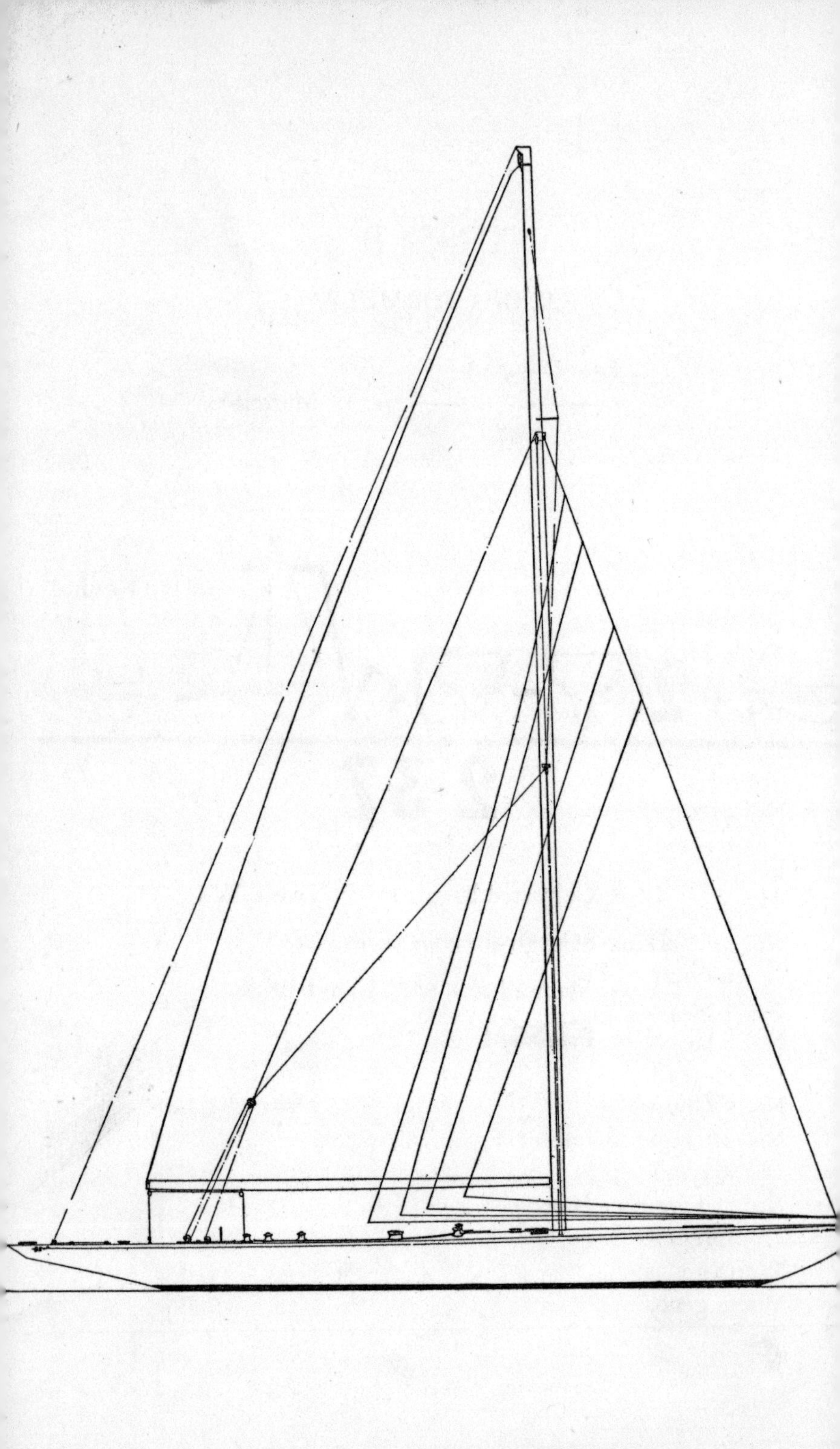

APPENDIX E

SAIL PLAN AND LIST OF SAILS

TYPE	WEIGHT OF CLOTH ozs./sq. yd.	LENGTH AT FOOT ft.	AREA sq. ft.
MAINSAILS			
Dacron	15	32	1,268
No. 2 Heavy	16¾	32	1,268
No. 3 Medium	16¾	32	1,268
No. 4 Light weather	14¾	32	1,268
Watts	13½	32	1,268
GENOAS			
No. 1 Large heavy genoa foresail	9¾	37′ 8″	1,100
No. 2 Large light genoa foresail	8½	37′ 8″	1,100
No. 5 Working genoa foresail	13¼	33	775
No. 7 Staysail	14¾	30	605
No. 8 Heavy spinnaker staysail	4	37′ 8″	440
No. 9 Ghoster	4	37′ 8″	1,100
No. 10 Light spinnaker staysail	2	35	470
No. 11 Large heavy genoa foresail	11¼	37′ 8″	1,100
Watts genoa	8	37′ 8″	1,100
Watts genoa	7	37′ 8″	1,100

APPENDIX E

LIST OF SAILS—*cont.*

TYPE	WEIGHT OF CLOTH ozs./sq. yd.	LENGTH AT FOOT ft.	AREA sq. ft.
SPINNAKERS			
Large heavy spinnaker A	2	71	approx. 3,750
Small heavy spinnaker B	2	50	,, 2,770
Reaching spinnaker C	4	56	2,365
Very light spinnaker D	1½	50	approx. 2,770
Large balloon spinnaker F	1½	92	5,570
Flat reaching spinnaker	4	51′ 6″	1,433
Herbulot spinnaker	1·6	72	4,100
Herbulot spinnaker (ex *Evaine*)	1·6	72	4,100

APPENDIX F

Key to perspective drawing between pages 100 and 101

1 Preventer backstay
2 Spinnaker sheet and brace blocks
3 Main sheet traveller
4 Navigator's plotting-table
5 Laminated plastic steering-wheel
6 Glass fibre and aluminium alloy bilge-pump
7 Removable bilge-pump handle
8 Main sheet winch
9 Runner winches
10 Spinnaker sheet and brace winches
11 Two-speed genoa sheet winches
12 Winch gear-boxes beneath cockpit floor
13 Canvas sleeve over winch drive shafts
14 Genoa tracks
15 Aluminium and balsa-wood laminate floor
16 Cooker (gas)
17 Lightweight toilet
18 Chain
19 Fresh water tank
20 Gas cylinder for cooker
21 Wash-basin
22 Spinnaker tack (fore-guy) winches
23 Spinnaker and jib halyard winches
24 Breakwater
25 Sleeping berths, port and starboard
26 Sleeping berth, port
27 Sail bin
28 Oilskin locker
29 Three pipecots in forecastle
30 Spinnaker-boom hoist
31 Streamlined high-tensile steel rigging (shrouds)
32 Spruce laid deck with marine plywood underlay
33 Tubular footrail with spinnaker foreguys inside
34 Fore hatch
35 Removable mooring bollard
36 Removable stem-head fitting
37 Aluminium alloy mast
38 Saloon stows flush in cabin floor
39 Sail hatch